MIRACLES
IN AMERICAN HISTORY
VOLUME TWO
Amazing Faith
that Shaped the Nation

SUSIE FEDERER
Adapted from William J. Federer's "American Minute"

Miracles in American History - Volume Two - Amazing Faith that Shaped the Nation
by Susie Federer
(adapted from William J. Federer's American Minute)

For other, contact: Amerisearch, Inc.
www.AmericanMinute.com smfederer@gmail.com
1-888-USA-WORD

HISTORY/RELIGIOUS/EDUCATION
ISBN 978-0-9896491-7-9

Cover design by Dustin Myers, longitudebranding.com

Amerisearch, Inc., PO Box 60442, Fort Myers, FL 33906
1-888-USA-WORD
www.AmericanMinute.com, smfederer@gmail.com

Because America needs miracles today ...

DEDICATION

I would like to dedicate this book to my amazing husband, William J. Federer. I call him my "Walking Encyclopedia" because he seems to remember every date, person and event in world history. He is truly amazing and a really nice guy too! I would know after 38 years of marriage. I love you, Honey.

Listening to Bill over the years has inspired me to share the miraculous stories in American history where God really moved. I pray that we inspire Miracles in your life.

I would also like to dedicate this book to my wonderful children and grandchildren, and any more to come. Thank You, Lord! You are so Faithful.

- Susie Federer, July 4, 2019

CONTENTS

INTRODUCTION

As I read through the hundreds of American history stories collected by my husband, it occurred to me that people of great faith prayed and BELIEVED for these miracles! So in this volume, I decided to focus on the amazing faith of people who shaped the development of our great nation.

Revivals happened at key times to bring Americans back to living for their beliefs in Christ so that God could use them to redirect the country. These people were not perfect but they obeyed God's calling on their lives and believed "they could do anything through Christ who strengthened them." (Phil. 4:13) Many gave thanks to the power of God's Holy Spirit.

Minorities rose from poverty and made a great difference in America because of their faith. Acceptance of others and loving them with the love of Jesus was crucial.

Missionaries were sent out from America to share the Gospel and enlighten the world. Then technology developed and God used ministers to broadcast the Good News of Salvation around the earth via radio, television, and the internet, and helped empower others to do so. I also include stories of leaders of faith in this century who have affected the world,

America went through many crises but God raised up leaders to bring her back under His Will. This is our time to lead!

℞

WILLIAM PENN GIVEN 45, 000 SQUARE MILES IN AMERICA – NAMES THE CAPITOL "CITY OF BROTHERLY LOVE"

The Invincible Spanish Armada was defeated by the English and Dutch in 1588. Afterwards, England and the Dutch grew to have colonial world empires which fought each other from the Far East to America, largely over control of the spice trade.

Meanwhile, an English Civil War resulted in the death of King Charles I, followed by a short–lived English Commonwealth under Oliver Cromwell. An officer gaining fame in the British Navy was Admiral William Penn. Cromwell sent Penn to the Caribbean where he captured Jamaica from the Spanish in 1655.

When Cromwell died, Admiral Penn helped restore Charles II to his father's throne in 1660, ending the English Commonwealth. A grateful Charles II knighted Penn, giving him the rank of Lord High Admiral with the title "Sir."

The Second Anglo–Dutch War took place 1665–1667. Admiral Sir William Penn again helped defeat the Dutch navy. This resulted in Britain capturing the Dutch colonies of New Amsterdam, which was renamed New York; and land that had previously been New Sweden, which would become Delaware, New Jersey and Pennsylvania.

Sir William Penn had high hopes for his son, also named William Penn, who served as a messenger between himself and the King. When young Penn was around 15 years old, his father was in the Caribbean. A Quaker missionary named Thomas Loe visited the Penn estate and shared about the light of the indwelling of the Holy Spirit. Penn later recalled that it was at this time that "the Lord visited me and gave me divine Impressions of Himself."

The younger Penn attended Oxford University, and being from an aristocratic family, belonged to the prestigious group of "Cavaliers." When the restored British government began enforcing religious uniformity, young Penn became critical of the King's church and began associating with the Quaker movement.

In England, from the time of Henry VIII, the King was the head of the Anglican Church, and subjects were required for most of 1535–1829 to take the Oath of Supremacy:

> I (state your name) do utterly testify and declare in my Conscience, that the King's Highness is the only Supreme Governor of this Realm ... in all Spiritual or Ecclesiastical things ... So help me God.

Not to take the Oath of Supremacy was considered treason, resulting in government prosecution, fines, arrest, imprisonment, and in extreme cases, being hanged, drawn and quartered, beheaded, or burned at the stake.

Numerous times the young Penn was arrested, and his father, Admiral Sir William Penn, used his influence to get him freed from jail. Penn urged his father: "I entreat thee not to purchase my liberty." His actions caused embarrassment to his father, who had spent his career carefully avoiding political entanglements. At one point, when young Penn publicly embraced Quaker beliefs, his father beat him with a cane, drove him out of the house and threatened to disinherit him.

Young Penn fled England and lived in France for several years. He met and traveled with George Fox (1624–1691), the founder of the Quakers. Penn returned to England and wrote *The Sandy Foundation Shaken,* which was critical of the King's Church.

In 1668, when the government tried to force Penn to deny his conscience and abandon his religious convictions, he refused, resulting in him being imprisoned in the Tower of London for eight months. Guards gave him pen and paper, thinking he wanted to write a recantation of his beliefs, but instead, Penn wrote his famous work *No Cross, No Crown:*

> Christ's cross is Christ's way to Christ's crown ... The unmortified Christian and the heathen are of the same religion, and the deity they truly worship is the god of this world. It is a false notion that they may be children of God while in a state of disobedience to his holy commandments, and disciples of Jesus though they revolt from his cross.

Upon being freed, Penn argued on behalf of the thousands of persecuted Quakers. In *Bushel's Case,* 1670, Penn was arrested and tried. When the jury came back with a not guilty verdict, the judge put the entire jury in jail.

While in London's notorious Newgate Prison, William Penn wrote 1670:

> By Liberty of Conscience, we understand not only a mere Liberty of the Mind ... but the exercise of ourselves in a visible way of worship, upon our believing it to be indispensably required at our hands, that if we neglect it for fear or favor of any mortal man, we sin, and incur divine wrath.

Penn wrote in *England's Present Interest Considered*, 1675: "Force makes hypocrites, 'tis persuasion only that makes converts."

Admiral Penn realized after his death there would be no one to intercede for his son, so he spent his final days securing a promise from King Charles II to be favorable to his son. Among his last correspondence, the Admiral wrote to his son: "Let nothing in this world tempt you to wrong your conscience."

Admiral Penn died in 1670, after which young Penn wanted to use his inheritance to buy West Jersey in America – land previously part of New Sweden before being taken over by the Dutch, and then by the English. His hope was to let persecuted Quakers emigrate there.

On June 24, 1680, Penn asked King Charles II for permission to purchase land, but to his surprise the King gave him a grant of land recently acquired from the Dutch and Swedes – 45,000 square miles, making Penn the largest non-royalty landowner in the world.

The Charter that King Charles II signed and gave to Penn on March 4, 1681, stated:

> Whereas our trusty and well-beloved subject, William Penn, esquire, son and heir of Sir William Penn, deceased, out of a commendable desire to enlarge our English Empire ... and also to reduce the savage natives by gentle and just manners to the love of civil society and Christian religion, hath humbly besought leave of us to transport an ample colony unto ... parts of America not yet cultivated and planted.

William Penn named his capitol city Philadelphia, Greek for city of "brotherly love."

CR

PENN'S HOLY EXPERIMENT "THE SEED OF A NATION" TO PRESERVE TRUE CHRISTIAN LIBERTY: — WHERE THE DECLARATION & THE CONSTITUTION WERE SIGNED

King Charles named this enormous amount of land, 29 million acres, "Pennsylvania" in honor of the father, Admiral Sir William Penn. Penn wanted to make his colony of Pennsylvania a "holy experiment" where Christians of different denominations who were persecuted in Europe for conscience sake, could flee for refuge and live together.

While most countries demanded that citizens believe as the government dictated, this colony allowed Christians, Jews, and others who believed in God to live together in religious toleration. This was an unprecedented endeavor in the world, taking place at a time in history when most of Europe was ruled by kings, China was ruled by emperors of the Qing dynasty, and Turkish Sultan Mehmed IV's 200,000 Ottoman Muslim soldiers were laying siege to Vienna, Austria.

On January 1, 1681, Penn wrote to a friend concerning the land given to him, declaring he would: "Make and establish such laws as shall best preserve true Christian and civil liberty, in all opposition to all unchristian ... practices."

"Philadelphia," city of "Brotherly Love," demonstrated Penn's tolerance. Not only were

Quakers allowed in, but Presbyterians, Lutherans, Baptists, Moravians, Mennonites, and Amish. Pennsylvania was one of the few colonies to allow in Catholics and Jews.

Pennsylvania's first legislative act was The Great Law of Pennsylvania, December 7, 1682:

> No person ... who shall confess and acknowledge one Almighty God to be the Creator, Upholder and Ruler of the World ... shall in any case be molested or prejudiced for his, or her Conscientious persuasion or practice but shall freely and fully enjoy his or her Christian Liberty without any interruption.

Penn insisted on treating Delaware Indians honestly, paying them a fair sum for their land. This resulted in Philadelphia being spared Indian attacks and scalpings that other colonies experienced. Before arriving, Penn wrote to the Delaware Indian chiefs, August 18, 1681:

> My Friends, There is one great God and Power that hath made the world and all things therein, to whom you and I and all people owe their being and well-being, and to whom you and I must one day give an account, for all that we do in the world;

> This great God hath written His law in our hearts by which we are taught and commanded to love and help and do good to one another and not to do harm ...

> Now this great God hath pleased to make ... the king of the country where I live ... [give] unto me a great province therein, but I desire to enjoy it with your love and consent, that we may always live together as neighbors and friends, else what would the great God say to us, who hath made us not to devour and destroy one another, but to live soberly and kindly together in the world ...

I have great love and regard towards you, and I desire to gain your love and friendship by a kind, just and peaceable life, and the people I send are of the same mind ...

I shall shortly come to you myself at which time we may more freely and largely confer and discourse of these matters. Receive those presents and tokens which I have sent to you as a testimony to my goodwill to you and my resolution to live justly, peaceably and friendly with you. I am your loving friend, William Penn.

Penn wrote in his *Concessions to the Province of Pennsylvania,* July 11, 1681:

Whatever is sold to the Indians, in consideration of their furs, shall be sold in the market place, and there suffer the test, whether good or bad; if good, to pass; if not good, not to be sold for good, that the natives may not be abused ... That no man shall ... affront, or wrong any Indian ... He shall incur the same penalty of the law, as if he had committed it against his fellow planter ...

If any Indian shall abuse ... any planter ... that he shall not be his own judge upon the Indian ... he shall make his complaint to the governor ... who shall ... take care with the king (chief) of the said Indian, that all reasonable satisfaction be made to the said injured planter ...

All differences, between the planters and the natives, shall also be ended by twelve men, that is, by six planters and six natives; that so we may live friendly together ...

Indians shall have liberty to do all things relating to improvement of their ground, and providing sustenance for their families, that any of the planters shall enjoy.

Lenape Delaware Indian Chief Tamanend gave his last message before dying in 1697:

> We and Christians of this river have always had a free roadway to one another, and though sometimes a tree has fallen cross the road, yet we have removed it again and kept the path clear.

Penn wrote in his *Charter of Privileges for Pennsylvanians,* 1701:

> Because no people can be truly happy though under the greatest enjoyments of civil liberties if abridged of the freedom of their consciences as to their religious profession and worship.

Instead of the harsh corporal punishment, Penn promoted the idea of putting a criminal in a room with a Bible until he "repents." Chuck Colson wrote in 1981:

> Quakers introduced the concept in Pennsylvania ... The first American prison was established in Philadelphia when the Walnut Street Jail was converted into a series of solitary cells where offenders were kept in solitary confinement. The theory was that they would become "penitents," confessing their crimes before God and thereby gaining a spiritual rehabilitation. Hence, the name "penitentiary" – as a place for penitents.

On a visit back to England, Penn met young Peter the Great of Russia, who was touring Europe to study methods of ship building. Peter attended a Quaker "Friends" meeting. William Penn wrote to Peter the Great, July 2, 1698:

> It was a profound respect, and not a vain curiosity, Great Czar, which brought me twice to wait upon thee. My desire was, and is, that as God Almighty has

distinguished thee above so many millions of thy fellow–creatures, so thou mayest distinguish thyself above them by an extraordinary zeal for piety and charity which are the two legs the Christian Religion stands upon ... If thou wouldst rule well, thou must rule for God; and to do that, thou must be ruled by Him ...

Know, great Czar, and take it with thee as one part of the collection of knowledge thou art making in this unexampled travel that 'tis in this kingdom of England that God has visited and touched the hearts of a people, above forty years ago, by the holy light and at grace of his Son and our Savior Jesus Christ.

By which their minds have been turned from false worship and evil living to worship God, who is a spirit, in and by his own Spirit.

William Penn died on July 30, 1718. More arrived in his colony: Quakers, Mennonites, Pietists, Amish, Anabaptists, Lutherans, Reformed, Moravians, Scots–Irish Presbyterians, Dunkers (German Baptist), Brethren, Schwenckfelders, French Huguenots, and other Protestant Christians.

The oldest church in Philadelphia is Old Swedes' Gloria Dei Church, which was begun by Lutheran missionary Johannes Campanius in 1646 among Swedish and Finnish settlers.

Johannes Campanius translated the very first book published in the Algonquin Indian language, Martin Luther's Small Catechism.

Penn's religious tolerance allowed the church to continue, and they erected their present building in 1698. In 1695, the Merion Friends (Quaker) Meeting House was built. It is the oldest church building in Pennsylvania and second oldest Friends meeting house in America.

In 1695, Philadelphia's Christ Church was built. It is called "the Nation's Church" as George Washington, Betsy Ross, Benjamin and Deborah Franklin, and their daughter, Sarah Franklin Bache, worshiped there. Others who worshiped at Christ Church included signers of the Declaration of Independence: John Adams, Benjamin Rush, Francis Hopkinson, Joseph Hewes, Robert Morris, James Wilson and George Ross.

From 1700 to 1750, Britain's laws against dissenters drove some 200,000 Scots and Scots–Irish Presbyterians from Scotland and Ireland to America. Most settled in Pennsylvania's Cumberland Valley and in the western counties of Lehigh, Bucks and Lancaster.

In 1711, Old Trinity Episcopal Church was built in Philadelphia. Beginning in 1720, German and Swiss settlers known as New Baptists, or Dunkers, began arriving in Pennsylvania, together with Anabaptists, Mennonites and Amish. Then arrived Protestant Schwenkfelders from Germany's Rhine Valley, Alsatia, Suabia, Saxony, and the Palatinate.

In 1732, the Seventh Day Dunkers (German Baptist Brethren) built Ephrata Cloister near Philadelphia. They had the second German printing press in America. They published "Martyrs Mirror," the largest book printed in America prior to the Revolutionary War, listing Christian martyrs from Christ until 1660.

Between 1730 and 1740, numerous Lutheran, Reformed, Brethren, and German Baptists congregations were formed in Pennsylvania, sometimes sharing the same buildings, Sunday Schools and ministers.

Rev. Richard Denton brought the Presbyterian faith to America in 1644. In 1692, just ten years after the arrival of William Penn, the first Presbyterian Church was organized in

Philadelphia, in a building called "Barbados Warehouse," being shared with Baptists and Congregationalists.

In 1704, Philadelphia's First Presbyterian Church moved to the corner of Bank Street and High Street (Market), where they built their first building. Members of the church included signers of the Declaration of Independence: James Wilson, Dr. Benjamin Rush, and Thomas McKean. In 1706, the first synod meeting of Presbyterian leaders in America took place in Philadelphia, led by Rev. Francis Makemie.

On May 21, 1789, the first General Assembly of the Presbyterian Church in America was held there. The first sermon at that assembly was preached by John Witherspoon, the president of Princeton University and a Signer of the Declaration of Independence.

In 1807, the first African Presbyterian Church was founded by former slave John Gloucester. At the time of the Revolution: 98 percent of the country was Protestant; around 1 percent Catholic; and one-tenth of one percent Jewish.

There were only seven Jewish congregations in the colonies prior to the Revolution, and two of those were in Pennsylvania: Mikveh Israel, begun in Philadelphia in 1740; and Shaarai Shomayim begun in Lancaster in 1747.

The first Jews in America were Sephardic, having fled from Spain, to Portugal, to South America and the West Indies. From the West Indies, Sephardic Jews came to the colonies of North America, the first of which was New Amsterdam, which became New York. When the British captured New York in 1776, many Jews fled to Philadelphia, where the Mikveh Israel congregation built the first synagogue in 1782.

Contributors to the building fund included Benjamin Franklin, Robert Morris, and Haym Solomon–Polish Jew financier of the American Revolution. In 1845, Rabbi Isaac Leeser of Mikveh Israel synagogue produced the first Jewish translation of the Bible in English published in the United States. When Mikveh Israel synagogue burned in 1872, Philadelphia's Christ Church contributed to rebuild it. The two congregations have a long custom of sharing a fellowship–dinner once a year which alternates between their two buildings.

In 1795, the first Ashkenazic Jewish synagogue in the Western Hemisphere was founded in Philadelphia, Congregation Rodeph Shalom.

After England's Reformation in 1534, there were no "English–speaking" Catholic Churches until St. Joseph Catholic Church was founded in 1731 in Philadelphia by 22 Irish and 15 Germans. It was the only place in the entire British Empire where a public Catholic church service took place legally. During the Revolution, French Generals Marquis de Lafayette and Comte de Rochambeau worshiped there.

Throughout the colonial era, Catholics were mostly in just two colonies: Maryland and Pennsylvania. Bishop John Carroll, founder of Georgetown University and cousin of Charles Carroll, a signer of the Declaration, wrote to Rome in 1790:

> The thirteen provinces of North America rejected the yoke of England, they proclaimed, at the same time, freedom of conscience ... Before this great event, the Catholic faith had penetrated two provinces only, Maryland and Pennsylvania. In all the others the laws against Catholics were in force.

Quakers and Mennonites led Pennsylvania to be the first in the nation to pass legislation to end slavery. America's first abolition society, The Society for the Relief of Free Negroes Unlawfully Held in Bondage, was founded in Philadelphia in 1775. After the Revolutionary War, it was reorganized in 1784 with Benjamin Franklin as its first president.

Philadelphia is the birthplace of the Methodist Episcopal churches in America, with St. George's Church, built in 1769, being the denomination's oldest continuously used church in the world. John Wesley, the founder of Methodism, sent the church a communion chalice.

St. George's pastor was Francis Asbury, the first Methodist bishop. He traveled 270,000 miles on horseback preaching the Gospel. He discipled and ordained more than 4,000 ministers, including Absalom Jones, Richard Allen, and Harry Hosier.

Absalom Jones established the African Episcopal Church of St. Thomas in 1792, the oldest black Episcopal congregation in America. Richard Allen established the African Methodist Episcopal Church in 1794. "Black Harry" Hosier established the African Zoar Church in 1796. St. George's Church appointed Mary Thorne as the first woman class leader.

After receiving his Charter from King Charles II, William Penn wrote:

> It is a clear and just thing, and my God who has given it me through many difficulties, will, I believe, bless and make it the seed of a nation.

It was the seed of a nation, being where the Continental Congress met, the Declaration of Independence was signed, the U.S. Constitution was written, and where the nation's first Capital was located. Psalm 133:1 "Behold, how good and how pleasant it is for brethren to dwell together in unity!"

Père Marquette Braves the Mississippi

CR

PÈRE MARQUETTE BRAVES THE MISSISSIPPI, BELIEVING HE WAS SENT BY GOD TO ILLUMINATE NATIVE AMERICANS WITH THE LIGHT OF THE HOLY GOSPEL

Père Jacques Marquette, ("Père" is French for "Father"), who arrived in Quebec from France to be a missionary among the Indians. In 1673, Frontenac, the Governor General of New France, commissioned Père Marquette to explore the unknown Mississippi River.

Marquette traveled with French explorer Louis Joliet by canoe along the west coast of Lake Michigan. They canoed to Green Bay, up the lower Fox River, across Lake Winnebago, and up the upper Fox River. They then portaged their canoes two miles through marsh to the Wisconsin River, where their two Indian guides abandoned them, fearing "river monsters."

Marquette and Joliet canoed the Wisconsin River to the Mississippi River, where they traveled south to just below the Arkansas River, hesitating to go further for fear of entering Spanish Territory.

Being the first Europeans to explore the northern Mississippi, Jacques Marquette gave his account in *Voyage et De'couverte de Quelques Pays et Nations de l'Amerique Septemtrionale* (translated 1852, *The Jesuit Relations,* Volume LIX):

We came to ... the Folle Avoine (Menominee). I entered their river to go and visit these people to whom we preached the Gospel ... in consequence of which, there are several good Christians among them.

I told ... of my design to ... discover those remote nations, in order to teach them the mysteries of our holy religion. They ... did their best to dissuade me ... that I would meet nations who never show mercy to strangers, but break their heads without any cause ... They also said that the great river was very dangerous ... full of horrible monsters, which devoured men and canoes together; that there was even a demon, who ... swallowed up all who ventured to approach him ...

Marquette continued:

I thanked them for the good advice that they gave me, but told them that I could not follow it, because the salvation of souls was at stake, for which I would be delighted to give my life; that I scoffed at the alleged demon; that we would easily defend ourselves against those marine monsters ... After making them pray to God, and giving them some instructions, I separated from them.

Large fish could have existed in the Mississippi River as it had never been commercially fished. As recent as February 14, 2011, fisherman Kenny Williams of Vicksburg, MS, caught an alligator gar in the Mississippi River that "measured 8 feet, 5 inches long, weighed 327 pounds, and was 48 inches around," and had a double row of razor sharp teeth. (*FoxNews.com*, 2/21/11; *FieldandStream.com* 2/23/11): "Officials with the Mississippi Department of Wildlife, Fisheries and Parks (MDWFP) said it could be the largest alligator gar caught."

Père Jacques Marquette continued in *Voyage et De'couverte de Quelques Pays et Nations de l'Amerique Septemtrionale* (translated 1852, The Jesuit Relations, Volume LIX):

Here we are at Maskoutens. This word may, in Algonquin, mean "the Fire Nation" — which, indeed, is the name given to this tribe. Here is the limit of the discoveries which the French have made, for they have not yet gone any farther ...

No sooner had we arrived than we, Monsieur Joliet, and I, assembled the elders together; and he told them that he was sent by Monsieur our Governor to discover new countries, while I was sent by God to illumine them with the light of the holy Gospel.

He told them that, moreover, the Sovereign Master of our lives wished to be known by all the nations; and that in obeying His will I feared not the death to which I exposed myself in voyages so perilous.

He informed them that we needed two guides to show us the way; and we gave them a present, by it asking them to grant us the guides. To this they very civilly consented; and they also spoke to us by means of a present, consisting of a mat to serve us as a bed during our whole voyage ...

Père Marquette related another account:

On the 25th day of June we perceived on the water's edge some tracks of men, and a narrow and somewhat beaten path leading to a fine prairie. We stopped to examine it; and, thinking that it was a road which led to some village of savages, we resolved to go and reconnoiter it.

We therefore left our two canoes under the guard of our people, strictly charging them not to allow themselves to be surprised, after which Monsieur Joliet and I undertook this investigation — a rather hazardous one for two men who exposed themselves alone to the mercy of a barbarous and unknown people.

We silently followed the narrow path, and, after walking about two leagues, we discovered a village on the bank of the river, and two others on a hill distant about half a league from the first. Then we heartily commended ourselves to God, and, after imploring His aid, we went farther without being perceived, and approached so near that we could even hear the savages talking.

We therefore decided that it was time to reveal ourselves. This we did by shouting with all our energy, and stopped without advancing any farther.

On hearing the shout, the savages quickly issued from their cabins, and having probably recognized us as Frenchmen, especially when they saw a black gown — or, at least, having no cause for distrust, as we were only two men, and had given them notice of our arrival — they deputed four old men to come and speak to us.

Two of these bore tobacco pipes, finely ornamented and adorned with various feathers. They walked slowly, and raised their pipes toward the sun, seemingly offering them to it to smoke—without, however, saying a word. They spent a rather long time in covering the short distance between their village and us.

Finally, when they had drawn near, they stopped to consider us attentively. I was reassured when I observed these ceremonies, which with them are performed only among friends; and much more so when I saw them clad in cloth, for I judged thereby that they were our allies.

I therefore spoke to them first, and asked who they were. They replied that they were Illinois; and, as a token of peace, they offered us their pipes to smoke. They afterward invited us to enter their village, where all the people impatiently awaited us.

On their return trip up the Illinois River, Jacques Marquette founded a mission among the Illinois Indians. The next year, caught by a winter storm, Jacques Marquette and two companions erected a rough log cabin near the shore of Lake Michigan.

A monument erected by the Illinois Society Daughters of Colonial Wars is inscribed:

On December 4, 1674, Père Jacques Marquette, S.J., and two voyageurs built a shelter near the mouth of the Chicago River. They were the first Europeans to camp here, the site of Chicago.

In 1675, just prior to his death, Père Jacques Marquette preached to several thousand Indians, as written in an account by Father Claude Dablon of the Society of Jesus, 1678:

Five hundred chiefs and old men, seated in a circle around the father, while the youth stood without to the number of fifteen hundred, not counting women and children who are very numerous ...

The father explained to them the principal mysteries of our religion, and the end for which he had come to their country; and especially he preached to them Christ crucified, for it was the very eve of the great day on which he died on the cross for them.

On May 18, 1675, being weakened and ill, Marquette died at the age of 37. He had founded Sault Ste. Marie, the first European settlement in Michigan, and the town of St. Ignace. Named after Marquette are a river, mountain, island, diocese, towns, townships, cities, counties, parks, schools, and Marquette University in Milwaukee, Wisconsin.

Père Marquette State Park near Grafton, IL, oversees the Illinois River close to where in joins the Mississippi River. In 1895, the State of Wisconsin placed a statue of Père Jacques Marquette in the U.S. Capitol Statuary Hall.

CR

GREAT FAITH OF THE MORAVIAN MISSIONARIES & THE 100 YEAR REVIVAL

"As one small candle may light a thousand, so the light here kindled hath shone unto many, yea in some sort to our whole nation," wrote Pilgrim Governor Bradford. An example of "one small candle" lighting "a thousand" occurred in the early 1700s, with a rich young ruler.

Count Nikolaus Ludwig von Zinzendorf was born in 1700 into a noble German family, with his ancestor being Maximillian I, the Holy Roman Emperor from 1508 to 1519. When he was six weeks old, his father died. When he was four years old, his mother remarried and he was sent off to live with his pietistic Lutheran grandmother, Henriette Catharina von Gersdorff.

In 1719, at the age of 19, Count Zinzendorf went on his "Grand Tour" – a trip where young aristocrats made their first introductions to the royal courts of France, the Netherlands, and major German kingdoms.

While on this tour, in the city of Dusseldorf, Count Zinzendorf visited a museum, where he viewed a painting by Domenico Feti depicting Christ's suffering. The painting, titled "Ecce Homo" ("Behold the Man"), had a Latin caption underneath, "Ego pro te haec passus sum, Tu vero quid fecisti pro me," which translated is: "This have I suffered for you; now what will you do for me?"

Young Count Zinzendorf was moved in a profound way. Convicted in his heart by the Holy Spirit, he came to an intensely personal faith in Christ, an experience which was part of a revival movement labeled "Pietism."

Zinzendorf became friends with Lutheran Pastors Johann Andreas Rothe of Berthelsdorf and Melchior Schäffer of Görlitz. They, together with friend Friedrich von Watteville, sought to spread a religious revival movement similar to that led by Jan Hus three centuries earlier.

In 1722, at the age of 22, Count Ludwig "Lewis" von Zinzendorf opened up his Berthelsdorf estate in Saxony to be a place of refuge for persecuted Christians of Moravia and Bohemia (area of the Czech Republic) who were displaced after religious conflicts of the Thirty Years War.

On a corner of his estate, Zinzendorf helped refugees build a village called "Herrenhut," meaning "The Lord's watchful care." Disagreements and discord almost ended this experiment of Christian unity, but 27-year-old Zinzendorf led them in a communion prayer service on August 13, 1727, where they forgave each other.

The prayer went on all day and all night, then, as they took turns with chores, the meeting continued 24 hours a day, seven days a week, month after month, year after year, uninterrupted for over 100 years.

Count Zinzendorf stated: "I have one passion: it is Jesus, Jesus only."

More Moravian missionaries were sent out from Herrenhut in the next 20 years than all Christendom had sent in the previous 200 years. Noted for being the first Protestant denomination to minister to slaves, Moravian missionaries went to:

- Greenland, Canada, Alaska;
- Inuit of Labrador;
- West Indies, Costa Rica, Belize, Haiti;
- American Indians, such as Cherokee, Lenape, Mohican, Algonquin;
- Northern shores of the Baltic;
- Slaves of South Carolina;
- Slaves in South America, Suriname, French Guyana, Peru;
- Tranquebar and Nicobar Islands in the East Indies;
- Copts in Egypt;
- Northern India and Nepal;
- Kenya, Rwanda, Zanzibar, Uganda, Sierra Leone, Tanzania, Kivu, Katanga in the Congo, and the west coast of South Africa.

In 1741, Count Zinzendorf visited America and met with leaders, including Ben Franklin. He hoped to unify the various German Protestant churches.

On Christmas Eve, 1741, Count Zinzendorf founded Bethlehem, Pennsylvania.

There his daughter, Benigna, organized a school which became Moravian College. He spent seven weeks traveling the wilderness with the German Indian agent and interpreter Conrad Weiser, to share his faith with Iroquois Indian chieftains.

He was the first person of European nobility to meet with Indian chiefs. Frederick C. Johnson wrote in the 1894 report, *Count Zinzendorf and The Moravian and Indian Occupancy of the Wyoming Valley,* (Pennsylvania) 1742–1763:

> The Delawares called themselves Lenni Lenape, signifying "original people" ...

> While on the way from Philadelphia to Bethlehem, Zinzendorf had felt drawn by some irresistible influence to go to Tulpehocken ("land of the turtles" near Reading, PA), where dwelt his interpreter and guide, Conrad Weiser, who was to accompany him to the Susquehanna ...

> Here he met the deputies of the Six Nations, then on their return from their conference with Governor George Thomas in regard to the Delawares remaining east of the Blue mountain ...

> The Count (Zinzendorf) became acquainted with the chiefs, gained their good will, and ratified a covenant with them in behalf of the (Moravian) Brethren as their representative; and a belt of wampum was given him as a token of their friendship , which was used ever afterwards in the dealings of the Moravians with the Iroquois.

> By this treaty the Count (Zinzendorf) believed the way would be opened for the spread of the gospel among the Northern Indians ...

His hope of Christianizing the fierce warriors of the northern border was not realized, but the Moravians would never have been able to accomplish as much as they did among the Delawares and Mohicans if they had not secured by this interview the amity of those who held sway over the enfeebled clans near the sea coast.

The Diary of Moravian Brother John Martin recorded:

1744. April 13th ... We immediately found the Chikasaw Indian, Chickasi, with whom we had been acquainted two years ago when Brother Lewis Zinzendorf was there. He was very friendly toward us and gave us something to eat.

He asked where Brother Lewis (Ludwig von Zinzendorf) and his daughter were. I told him they were gone to Europe. He asked if they arrived safe there. I said yes. He was much rejoiced at that. He said he had thought much on him and his daughter.

We lodged with his cousin, who received us in much love and friendship and gave us of the best he had ... How often did I call to mind how Brother Lewis (Ludwig von Zinzendorf) said at that time:

"The Shawanese Indians will all remove in a short time, and our Savior will bring another people here who shall be acquainted with His wounds, and they shall build a City of Grace there to the honor of the Lamb."

How my heart rejoiceth now at the thoughts of it because I see that everything is preparing for it ...

The Diary of Moravian Brother John Martin continued:

We visited carefully all the places where our tent had been pitched two years ago, and where so many tears had been shed. The Lamb has numbered them all and put them in His bottle. (Psalm 56:8) We stayed there four days. The Indians loved us. Our walk and behavior preached amongst them and showed that we loved them.

They could heartily believe and realize that we had not come amongst them for our own advantage, but out of love to them. We visited them often.

I asked the Indian with whom we were acquainted, if they would like a brother whom they loved much to come and live amongst them some time or other, and tell them sometimes of our great God who loved mankind so much? They answered yes, they should be very glad.

The Moravian Historical Society has preserved records of many Moravian missionaries, such as David Zeisberger and Conrad Weiser. One account read how the Indians:

In times of scarcity, flocked to Gnadenhutten (House of Grace), professing Christianity and filling themselves at the tables of the pious missionaries. When the season for hunting came, they would return to the wilderness in the pursuit of game, and with the profits of the chase would procure liquor from heartless traders. Some, however, were sincere in their professions and died in the faith.

The Moravian missionaries were given Indian names, and proclaimed the Gospel on both branches of the Susquehanna, on the Lackawanna and throughout northeastern Pennsylvania wherever the smoke ascended from the rude bark wigwam.

Another account read:

In October, 1748, Baron John de Watteville, a bishop of the Moravian Church, son-in-law and principal assistant of Count Zinzendorf, arrived from Europe on an official visit, and one of the first things he undertook was a visit to the Indian country ...

"Exploring the lovely valley which opened to their view, they found the plain of Skehantowano, where Zinzendorf's tent had first been pitched; the hill where God had delivered him from the fangs of the adder (snake), and the spot where the Shawanese had watched him with murderous design.

The very tree was still standing on which he had graven the initials of his Indian name. Among the inhabitants, however, many changes had taken place. The majority of the Shawanese had gone to the Ohio, and but few natives of any other tribe remained, with the exception of Nanticokes.

Watteville faithfully proclaimed the Gospel, and on the 7th of October was celebrated the Lord's Supper, the first time the holy sacrament was administered in the Wyoming Valley (Pennsylvania).

The hymns of the little company swelled solemnly through the night, while the Indians stood listening in silent awe at the doors of their wigwams. And when they heard the voice of the stranger lifted up in earliest intercession, as had been Zinzendorf's voice in that same region six years before, they felt that the white man was praying that they might learn to know his God."

Zinzendorf's interpreter, Conrad Weiser, married his daughter to a young pietist German minister named Henry Muhlenberg, who is considered one of the founders of the Lutheran Church in America. He became pastor of fifty German families at the Old Trappe Church in Pennsylvania, December 12, 1742. In 1751, he founded Trinity Lutheran Church in Reading, Pennsylvania.

Pietist was a movement within Lutheranism which stressed a personal relationship with Christ and a separation from that which was worldly, such as bars, theater, brothels, and politics. This developed into the political attitude of "separation of church and state."

Puritan Calvinists, on the other hand, believed God's will applied to everything: one's life, marriage, family, church and government. It was the duty of Christians to put everything including government, in line with God's will.

It was therefore a drastic step for Henry Muhlenberg's son, John Peter Muhlenberg, pastor of Emanuel Church in Woodstock, Virginia, to join General George Washington's army as a colonel, with 300 members of his church forming the 8th Virginia Regiment.

John Peter Muhlenberg was promoted to Major–General in the Continental Army, then elected to the U.S. Congress and Senate.

Henry Muhlenberg's other son, Frederick Augustus Muhlenberg, was pastor of a pietist Lutheran congregation in New York. At first, Frederick rebuked his brother, John Peter: "You have become too involved in that, which as a preacher, you have nothing whatsoever to do."

When the British invaded New York and burned Frederick's church, he had a change of heart and got involved. Frederick Muhlenberg went on to be elected the first Speaker of the U.S. House of Representatives.

Both John Peter and Frederick were members of the First Session of U.S. Congress which passed twelve amendments limiting the power of the Federal Government, of which ten were ratified by the States. Obviously, they did not think the First Amendment was intended to keep pastors from being involved in politics.

Their father, Henry Muhlenberg, died October 7, 1787. He had written of General George Washington at Valley Forge in *The Notebook of a Colonial Clergyman*:

> I heard a fine example today, namely that His Excellency General Washington rode around among his army yesterday and admonished each to fear God, to put away wickedness ... and to practice Christian virtues ... From all appearances General Washington does not belong to the so–called world of society, for he respects God's Word, believes in the atonement through Christ, and bears himself in humility and gentleness.
>
> Therefore, the Lord God has also singularly, yea, marvelously preserved him from harm in the midst of countless perils, ambuscades, fatigues, etc., and has hitherto graciously held him in His hand as a chosen vessel.

ॐ

WESLEYS & "THE RELIGION OF THE HEART" –THE FOUNDING OF GEORGIA

In 1735, a young Oxford graduate and named John Wesley was sent as the Anglican minister to the new American Colony of Georgia. He had hopes of evangelizing the Indians. His brother, Charles Wesley, was secretary to the colony's Governor, James Oglethorpe. Georgia was founded to give a second chance to those who had been in prison or who were persecuted for their faith.

On the trip from England to St. Simon Island, Georgia, their ship, the Simmonds, was also carrying a group of 25 German Moravian missionaries, as Wesley noted in his journal:

> Sunday, January 25, 1736. At seven I went to the Germans (Moravians). I had long before observed ... their humility ... by performing those servile offices for the other passengers, which none of the English would undertake ... saying ... "their loving Savior had done more for them" ... If they were pushed, struck, or thrown down, they rose again and went away; but no complaint was found in their mouth.

Suddenly, the ship was caught in a terrible storm which shredded the main sail and flooded the deck.

Wesley saw everyone panic in fear, except for the Moravian men, women and children, who continued to sing praise songs. He was struck on how their relationship with the Lord was closer than his, as he wrote in his journal:

> There was now an opportunity of trying whether they were delivered from the Spirit of fear ... In the midst of the psalm wherewith their service began, the sea broke over, split the main–sail in pieces, covered the ship, and poured in between the decks, as if the great deep had already swallowed us up. A terrible screaming began among the English.
>
> The Germans (Moravians) calmly sang on. I asked one of them afterwards, "Were you not afraid?" He answered, "I thank God, no." I asked, "But were not your women and children afraid?" He replied, mildly, "No; our women and children are not afraid to die."
>
> From them, I went to their crying, trembling neighbors, and pointed out to them the difference in the hour of trial, between him that feareth God, and him that feareth him not. At twelve the wind fell. This was the most glorious day which I have hitherto seen.

In Georgia, the Wesleys were unsuccessful in ministry and returned to England in 1737. They were befriended by another Moravian missionary, Peter Boehler, who was waiting for a ship to sail to Georgia. Boehler shared with the Wesleys regarding the indwelling of the Holy Spirit, which resulted in their "Aldersgate experience" in May of 1738.

John was touched by the Holy Spirit and had a profound conversion experience, writing "I felt my heart strangely warmed," realizing that God's grace was "free for all."

He wrote in his journal after the prayer service:

> I felt I did trust in Christ, Christ alone, for salvation; and an assurance was given me that He had taken away my sins, even mine, and saved me from the law of sin and death.

Later in 1738, John Wesley traveled to Moravia in eastern Germany where he lived and worshiped for several months with Count Ludwig von Zinzendorf and the Moravian believers, experiencing first hand their sincere Christianity, being "the religion of the heart."

Wesley wrote in his journal:

> God has given me, at length, the desire of my heart. I am with a church ... in whom is the mind of Christ, and who so walk as He walked ... As they all have one Lord and one faith, so they are partakers with one spirit, the spirit of meekness and love, which uniformly and continually animates all their conversation. Oh! How high and holy a thing Christianity is!

Wesley continued, contrasting the Moravian church with his previous church experience of works under the King's government:

> How widely different from that, I know not what, which is so called, though it neither purifies the heart, nor renews the life, after the image of our Blessed Redeemer.
>
> I grieve to think how that holy name by which we are called must be blasphemed

among the heathen, while they see discontented Christians, passionate Christians, resentful Christians, earthly–minded Christians.

Yea, to come to what we are apt to count small things, while they see Christians judging one another, ridiculing one another, speaking evil of one another, increasing instead of bearing one another's burdens.

John Wesley left Germany and returned to England, where he and his brother, Charles, began a revival movement within the Anglican Church called Methodism.

Charles Wesley wrote over 6,500 hymns, many of which are still sung.

John preached thousands of sermons and organized a system of itinerate preachers who traveled through shires and towns in England in a circuit, or circle. He spoke of the inner witness of the presence of the Holy Spirit in one's heart, as:

> ... an inward impression on the soul of believers, whereby the Spirit of God directly testifies to their spirit that they are the children of God.

CR

WHITEFIELD & THE GREAT AWAKENING REVIVAL IN AMERICA

A friend of the Wesleys, George Whitefield, became one of the era's most notable preachers. He came to America seven times, preaching to thousands and befriending leaders such as Ben Franklin. Whitefield spoke at least 18,000 times to an estimated 10 million hearers in England and America.

George Whitefield had attended Oxford with John and Charles Wesley, who began the Methodist revival movement within the Anglican Church. In 1733, when he finally understood and believed the Gospel, George Whitefield exclaimed: "Joy—joy unspeakable—joy that's full of, big with glory!"

Beginning in 1740, George Whitefield preached seven times in America. He spread the Great Awakening Revival, which helped unite the Colonies prior to the Revolutionary War.

Whitefield's preaching stirred crowds with enthusiasm, which was criticized by the formal, established churches of the day. When they closed their doors to him, Whitefield began preaching out-of-doors. Crowds grew so large that no church could have held the number of people, sometimes being as large as 25,000.

Ben Franklin wrote in his *Autobiography* that George Whitefield's voice could be heard over 500 feet away:

> He preached one evening from the top of the Court–house steps ... Streets were filled with his hearers ... I had the curiosity to learn how far he could be heard by retiring backwards down the street ... and found his voice distinct till I came near Front–street.

Ben Franklin continued his description of evangelist George Whitefield:

> Multitudes of all denominations attended his sermons ... It was wonderful to see the change soon made in the manners of our inhabitants. From being thoughtless or indifferent about religion, it seemed as if all the world were growing religious, so that one could not walk thro' the town in an evening without hearing psalms sung in different families of every street.

Sarah Edwards, the wife of Jonathan Edwards, wrote to her brother in New Haven concerning the effects George Whitefield's ministry:

> It is wonderful to see what a spell he casts over an audience by proclaiming the simplest truths of the Bible ... Our mechanics shut up their shops, and the day laborers throw down their tools to go and hear him preach, and few return unaffected.

Ben Franklin helped finance the building of an auditorium in Philadelphia for George Whitefield to preach in, which was later donated as the first building of the University of Pennsylvania. A bronze statue of George Whitefield is located on the University's campus, in the Dormitory Quadrangle.

Franklin printed Whitefield's journal and sermons. Being Postmaster in Philadelphia, Franklin helped spread Whitefield's sermons through colonial America. In one sermon, George Whitefield proclaimed:

> Never rest until you can say, "the Lord our righteousness." Who knows but the Lord may have mercy, nay, abundantly pardon you? Beg of God to give you faith; and if the Lord give you that, you will by it receive Christ, with His righteousness, and His all ... None, none can tell, but those happy souls who have experienced it with what demonstration of the Spirit this conviction comes ...

Whitefield continued:

> Oh, how amiable, as well as all sufficient, does the blessed Jesus now appear! With what new eyes does the soul now see the Lord its righteousness! Brethren, it is unutterable ... Those who live godly in Christ, may not so much be said to live, as Christ to live in them ... They are led by the Spirit as a child is led by the hand of its father ... They hear, know, and obey His voice ... Being born again in God they habitually live to, and daily walk with God.

Whitefield's influence was so profound, that when war threatened with Spain and France, Franklin drafted and printed a General Fast for Pennsylvania, December 12, 1747.

In 1752, George Whitefield wrote to Benjamin Franklin, who had invented the lightning rod: "My Dear Doctor ... I find that you grow more and more famous in the learned world." Franklin wrote to Whitefield, 1764:

> Your frequently repeated wishes and prayers for my eternal as well as temporal happiness are very obliging. I can only thank you for them, and offer you mine in return.

In 1769, Whitefield wrote Franklin on the night before his last trip to America. In this last surviving letter, Whitefield shares his desire that both he and Franklin would: "... be in that happy number of those who in the midst of the tremendous final blaze shall cry Amen."

Franklin wrote to Whitefield:

> I sometimes wish you and I were jointly employed by the Crown to settle a colony on the Ohio ... a strong body of religious and industrious people! ... Might it not greatly facilitate the introduction of pure religion among the heathen, if we could, by such a colony, show them a better sample of Christians than they commonly see in our Indian traders?

George Whitefield died September 30, 1770. As he was dying, he declared: "How willing I would ever live to preach Christ! But I die to be with Him!"

Whitefield was one of the first ministers to publicly preach the Gospel to slaves. Though he advocated to improve the treatment of slaves, he sadly did not seek to end the institution.

He left his orphanage in Georgia to Selina Shirley, the Countess of Huntingdon, who had financially helped both Whitefield and John Wesley in the spread of Methodism. She financed the construction of 64 chapels in Wales and England, supported missions in Sierra Leone, Africa, and was the first female principal of Trefeca College in Wales, which educated Methodist ministers.

The Countess of Huntingdon was patron of the famous black female poet, Phillis Wheatley, who corresponded with John Newton, author of "Amazing Grace," and with General Washington, who was so impressed he met with her at his headquarters in Cambridge. Wheatley wrote in her poem "On the Death of the Rev. Mr. George Whitefield," 1770:

> He pray'd that grace in ev'ry heart might dwell, He long'd to see America excel."

Other ministers carried the flame of Whitefield's preaching, such as: Jonathan Edwards; William Tennent, and his son, Gilbert Tennent; Ebenezer Pemberton; James Davenport; Samuel Finley; Theodore Frelinghuysen, and missionary David Brainerd.

The Great Awakening Revival resulted in the churches of the country to become divided between very traditional "Old Lights," and the more enthusiastic "New Lights," from which were formed new universities, such as University of Pennsylvania, 1740; Princeton, 1746; Columbia. 1754; Brown, 1764; Rutgers, 1766; and Dartmouth, 1770.

In one of his sermons, George Whitefield declared:

> Would you have peace with God? Away, then, to God through Jesus Christ, who has purchased peace; the Lord Jesus has shed His heart's blood for this. He died for this; He rose again for this; He ascended into the highest heaven, and is now interceding at the right hand of God.

USA IOc

Molly Pitcher, Monmouth, 1778

CR

MOLLY PITCHER, BETSY ROSS, & COURAGEOUS WOMEN OF THE REVOLUTION –THE MOTTO: *"GOD, HOME & COUNTRY"*

Courageous women have always played a vital role in American history. Addressing the Daughters of the American Revolution, April 19, 1926, President Calvin Coolidge stated:

The importance of women in the working out the destiny of mankind ... As there were fathers in our Republic so there were mothers ... By their abiding faith they inspired and encouraged the men; by their sacrifice, they performed their part in the struggle out of which came our country ...

We read of the flaming plea of Hanna Arnett, which she made on a dreary day in December, 1776, when Lord Cornwallis, victorious at Fort Lee, held a strategic position in New Jersey. A group of Revolutionists, weary and discouraged, were discussing the advisability of giving up the struggle ...

Casting aside the proprieties which forbade a woman to interfere in the counsels of men, Hannah Arnett proclaimed her faith. In eloquent words, which at once shamed and stung to action, she convinced her husband and his companions that righteousness must win.

Women followed the American army to Valley Forge, enduring the freezing winter of 1777. Over 2,500 soldiers perished from hunger, typhoid, jaundice, dysentery, and pneumonia, but also an estimated 500 women died there. Coolidge continued:

> We have been told of the unselfish devotion of the women who gave their own
> warm garments to fashion clothing for the suffering Continental Army during that
> bitter winter at Valley Forge. The burdens of the war were not all borne by the men.

Referred to as "camp followers," these women were organized by Martha Washington, Lucy Knox, wife of Colonel Henry Knox, and Caty Greene, wife of General Nathanael Greene. To help the Continental Army, they scavenged for supplies, cooked food, washed clothes, formed sewing circles to knit and mended ragged uniforms and blankets, and cared for sick and dying soldiers. One of the ladies, Mrs. Westlake, described Martha Washington:

> I never in my life knew a woman so busy from early morning until late at night
> as was Lady Washington, providing comforts for the sick soldiers.

Esther DeBerdt Reed, wife of officer Joseph Reed, and Sarah Franklin Bache, daughter of Benjamin Franklin, organized "The Ladies of Philadelphia" and raised $300,000 for General Washington to buy warm clothes for American troops.

During the Revolution, many, like Lucy Knox, left their Loyalist British families who sailed for England, never to see them again, in order to join their patriotic American husbands on military assignments in shifting encampments.

Lucy and Colonel Henry Knox did not have a permanent home until they were married

20 years. President Calvin Coolidge continued:

> Who has not heard of Molly Pitcher, whose heroic services at the Battle of Monmouth helped the sorely tried army of George Washington!

Molly Pitcher is generally believed to be Mary Ludwig Hays. When her husband enlisted, she became one of the "camp followers."

During the intense heat of the battles, these women would go from trench to trench, carrying pitchers of water to the parched soldiers. Women also carried a continuous supply of water to those loading the cannons. Water was needed to cool and clean the hot barrels of the cannons between shots, using a soaked end of a long ramrod. If this was not done, the cannons would soon overheat and become useless.

At the Battle of Monmouth, June 28, 1778, Molly Pitcher was bringing water to soldiers, while her husband manned one of the cannons. When her husband collapsed from heat stroke, Mary took his place swabbing and loading the cannon for the rest of the battle.

A British cannonball flew between her legs, tearing off part of her skirt. Molly straightened up and uttered, "Well, that could have been worse," and resumed loading the cannon. Soldier Joseph Plumb Martin described:

> A woman whose husband belonged to the artillery and who was then attached to a piece in the engagement, attended with her husband at the piece the whole time.
>
> While in the act of reaching a cartridge and having one of her feet as far before the other as she could step, a cannon shot from the enemy passed directly between

her legs without doing any other damage than carrying away all the lower part of her petticoat.

Looking at it with apparent unconcern, she observed that it was lucky it did not pass a little higher, for in that case it might have carried away something else, and continued her occupation.

Hearing of her courage, General George Washington commended Mary Ludwig Hays, issuing her a warrant as a non-commissioned officer. She was known as "Sergeant Molly."

A similar story is that of Margaret Cochran Corbin, wife of artilleryman John Corbin. On November 16, 1776, John Corbin, along with 2,800 Continental soldiers, defended Manhattan's Fort Washington, which was being attacked by 9,000 Hessian mercenary troops.

Margaret Corbin was bringing water to swab the cannon, when her husband was killed. She immediately took his place at the cannon, and helped return fire. Seriously wounded in her arm, Margaret Corbin, or "Captain Molly," was the first woman in U.S. history to be awarded a military pension.

When the men of Pepperell, Massachusetts, went off to war, Prudence Cummings Wright and Sarah Shattuck formed their own militia of women to protect the remaining townspeople – "Mrs. David Wright's Guard."

Their weapons were everything from muskets to farm tools. Women managed homesteads while their husbands fought. They worked the farms, raised families, and defended against Indians stirred up by the British to attack.

Women raised money for suffering soldiers, organized resistance protests, boycotted British–made products, which meant going back to using their old spinning wheels. Women engaged in the riskier roles as messengers, scouts, saboteurs, or spies, the punishment for which, if caught, was hanging.

In addition to well-known names, such as Abigail Adams, Mercy Otis Warren, Dolley Madison, and Deborah Read Franklin, there were many others.

Catherine "Kate" Moore Barry, the "Heroine of the Battle of Cowpens," rode through the back trails of South Carolina to warn of approaching British troops and round up militia, including her husband, to join General Daniel Morgan for the Battle of Cowpens, January 17, 1781.

16-year-old Sybil Ludington, on the night of April 26, 1777, rode 40 miles through Putnam and Dutchess Counties waking up patriots to join the militia, led by her father, Colonel Henry Ludington. Sybil delivered the urgent warning that the British had burned Danbury, Connecticut, and were fast approaching.

Lydia Darragh, a Quaker, had her home commandeered by British officers for weeks. During their meetings, Lydia hid in a closet under the stairs and listened through the walls. Hearing their plans, she made notes on small pieces of paper and sewed them into button covers on her son's coat. She then told her son to go to General Washington's camp at Whitemarsh. This intelligence provided by Lydia Darragh saved Americans from a surprise British attack.

In September 1775, 22-year-old Deborah Champion risked her life to deliver an urgent message from her father, Henry Champion – the Continental Army's commissary general, to General George Washington. Hiding the important papers under the bodice of her linsey–woolsey dress, she disguised herself as an old woman, wearing a silk hood and an oversized bonnet, then rode past several British checkpoints between New London, Connecticut, and Boston.

Anna Smith Strong was an integral part of the Culper Spy Ring, which gathered information for General Washington, 1778–1781. Robert Townsend, pretending to be a loyalist, learned of British troops movements around New York and told tavern owner Austin Roe, who got it to Abraham Woodhull.

Woodhull was signaled by Anna Smith Strong, when she hung her laundry outside to dry on a clothesline in pre–arranged configurations, that Caleb Brewster was waiting in a cove to take the information across Long Island Sound to Major Ben Tallmadge and General Washington.

Hot tempered Nancy Hart had her cabin searched by six British soldiers. They shot her prized turkey and ordered her to cook it. While serving the soldiers wine, she discreetly passed their stacked muskets through a crack in the wall to her daughter outside.

When the soldiers finally noticed what she was doing, she pointed one of the guns at them saying that she would shoot the first one who moved, which she promptly did. Nancy held the rest at gun point until her husband arrived. She insisted they be hung. In 1912, railroad construction worker grading land near the old Hart cabin found a neat row of six skeletons.

Deborah Samson (or Sampson) Gannett, after being freed from being an indentured servant on a farm, bound her chest, dressed as a man, and enlisted in the Continental Army under the name Robert Shurtliff.

She served three years, being injured several times, but refused medical attention for fear of being found out. It was not until she became deathly ill of fever that the doctor discovered her identity. She was honorably discharged. In 1792, Deborah received back pay, and in 1805, Congress granted her a pension as a war veteran.

Martha Bratton, wife of Colonel William Bratton, blew up a cache of gunpowder to keep it from the British. When questioned, she proclaimed, "It was I who did it!" A British officer held a reaping hook to her throat, demanding she confess where her husband was, but Martha refused to tell. When a battle was taking place right outside her home, she extinguished the fire in the fireplace and put her little son up the chimney to keep him from being hit by stray gunfire.

Nancy "Nanyehi" Ward was a Cherokee in eastern Tennessee. Cherokee had sided with the British during the French and Indian War, and again during the Revolution. Nanye'hi learned that the British had incited her tribe to attack a nearby American settlement. She took the risk of freeing American prisoners so they could warn their village, one of whom, Lydia Bean, was expecting to be burned to death the next day. While a captive, Lydia Bean and Nanye'hi reportedly traded cooking advice, such as making butter.

Abigail Adams wrote to her husband, John, from their home in Braintree, Massachusetts,

October 16, 1774, regarding increased tensions with Great Britain:

> I dare not express to you, at three hundred miles distance, how ardently I long for your return ... And whether the end will be tragical, Heaven only knows. You cannot be, I know, nor do I wish to see you, an inactive spectator; but if the sword be drawn, I bid adieu to all domestic felicity, and look forward to that country where there are neither wars nor rumors of war, in a firm belief that through the mercy of its King we shall both rejoice there together ... Your most affectionate, Abigail Adams.

In a letter dated June 25, 1775, Abigail Adams wrote again to her husband regarding the battle at Charlestown, Massachusetts:

> We live in continual Expectation of Hostilities. Scarcely a day that does not produce some, but like Good Nehemiah having made our prayer with God, and set the people with their Swords, their Spears and their bows we will say unto them, Be not afraid of them. Remember the Lord who is great and terrible, and fight for your Brethren, your sons and your daughters, your wives and your houses ...

> They (British) delight on molesting us on the Sabbath. Two Sabbaths we have been in such Alarms that we have had no meetings. This day we have set under our own vine in quietness, have heard Mr. Taft, from Psalms. The Lord is good to all and his tender mercies are over all his works.

On January 2, 1952, the U.S. Postal Service issued a 3–cent stamp in Philadelphia to commemorate the 200th anniversary of the birth of Betsy Ross. She was born a day earlier,

January 1, 1752, to a Quaker family in Philadelphia. Quakers were also the first and strongest opponents of slavery in America. Betsy was the 8th of 17 children. She apprenticed as a seamstress and fell in love with upholsterer John Ross, the son of an Episcopal rector at Christ Church, and nephew of Declaration signer, George Ross.

George Ross, the son of an Anglican clergyman, was a delegate from Pennsylvania to the Constitutional Convention, being elected its first vice-president. He was a colonel in the Continental Army and later an admiralty judge in Pennsylvania where he refused to acknowledge the authority of the Federal court over State decisions.

George Ross' sister married George Read, another signer of the Declaration. John and Betsy eloped, as Quakers forbade interdenominational marriage. They were married by the last colonial Governor of New Jersey, William Franklin, the son of Ben Franklin.

John and Betsy Ross attended Christ's Church with: George Washington, Robert Morris, Francis Hopkins, Alexander Hamilton, Thomas Jefferson, and Benjamin Franklin. The Ross' pew, number 12, was next to a column adjoining George Washington's pew number 56 and not far from Ben Franklin's pew number 70.

During the Revolution, John Ross died when a munitions depot he was guarding blew up. Shortly after, in June 1776, Washington reportedly asked Betsy Ross to sew an American Flag, based on a design drawn up by Francis Hopkinson, a signer of the Declaration.

Another woman who made the Grand Union Flag of 1775 was Rebecca Flower Young, whose daughter Mary Young Pickersgill made the famous "Star Spangled Banner" which flew over Fort McHenry during the War of 1812.

A widow, Betsy Ross married sea captain Joseph Ashburn at the Old Swedes Church in 1777. That winter the British forcibly quartered in the home of Betsy and Joseph Ashburn.

Joseph Ashburn later sailed to the West Indies for war supplies, but was captured and sent to Old Mill Prison, where he died in 1782. Fellow prisoner John Claypoole later brought the news of Joseph's death to Betsy, only to fall in love with her himself.

Betsy married John Claypoole at Christ Church, May 8, 1783, and together they had 5 children. The Betsy Ross Bridge across the Delaware River connecting Philadelphia with Pennsauken, New Jersey, is named in her honor.

To continue the heroic legacy, the Daughters of the American Revolution was founded in 1890, and incorporated by an Act of Congress in 1896. Its motto is: "God, Home, and Country." Voicing the sentiment of the courageous, patriotic women of the Revolution, Abigail Adams wrote to her husband, September 16, 1775:

> And unto Him who mounts the whirlwind and directs the storm, I will cheerfully leave the ordering of my lot and whether adverse or prosperous days should be my future portion, I will trust in His right Hand to lead me safely through, and after a short rotation of events, fix me in a state immutable and happy ... Adieu! I need not say how sincerely I am your affectionate, Abigail Adams.

CR

FRANCIS ASBURY & THE CIRCUIT–RIDING PREACHERS
"PREACH AS IF YOU HAVE SEEN HEAVEN"

Francis Asbury was born August 20, 1745. As a teenager, he was inspired by the Wesleys and George Whitefield. At age 18, he became an Anglican Methodist lay minister. At the age 22, Francis Asbury was appointed by John Wesley to be a traveling preacher across England.

When George Whitefield died in 1771, the question arose as to who would follow in his footsteps and preach in America. Francis Asbury, at the age of 26, volunteered. In 1771, he arrived in America, and for the next 45 years, he road 300,000 miles on horseback, from the Atlantic to the Appalachians, from Maine to the Gulf of Mexico, spreading the Gospel.

Prior to the Revolution, the Anglican Church was the official established state church in: Virginia in 1609; New York in 1693; Maryland in 1702; South Carolina in 1706; North Carolina in 1730; and Georgia in 1758.

In English colonies, everyone paid taxes to the King's government, and the government paid the salaries of the Anglican pastors. Pastors lived on church–government owned farms called "glebes."

On July 9, 1776, patriots in New York pulled down the statue of King George. Several

American colonies made it an act of treason for pastors to continue saying public prayers for the King.

In 1777, British General Howe invaded Philadelphia and imprisoned Rev. Jacob Duche', the Anglican chaplain of the Continental Congress, and undoubtedly pressured him to abandon the American cause.

As the Revolution progressed, Anglican ministers faced a crisis of conscience. They had to choose between allegiance to the King and state, or allegiance to the patriotic American cause.

The problem was, if they joined with those fighting for independence, they would lose their means of livelihood. As a result, most Anglican ministers returned to England, but Francis Asbury was one of the few who chose to stay in America. He stated: "I can by no means agree to leave such a field for gathering souls to Christ as we have in America."

Francis Asbury preached over 16,000 sermons in churches, town squares and court houses, addressing everyone he met, from travelers to workers in the fields to laborers in tobacco houses. He rode an average of 6,000 miles a year.

In 1784, 81-year-old John Wesley appointed Francis Asbury and Thomas Coke as America's first Methodist bishops, being responsible to oversee the Methodist revival movement in the America.

The crisis of conscience for Anglican ministers came to a head in 1784, when Rev. Samuel Seabury of Connecticut sought consecration as an Anglican bishop but could not take the Oath of Supremacy to the King.

A Bishop in Scotland agreed to consecrate Rev. Seabury, and in 1785, Bishop Seabury began ordaining ministers in Connecticut. This was the beginning of the official split of the Episcopal Church in America away from the Anglican Church of England.

Episcopal ministers, Rev. William Smith of Maryland and Rev. William White of Philadelphia, in 1786, proposed a revised Book of Common Prayer where references to the King were replaced with references to Congress.

Near that same time, at the Baltimore Christmas Conference in 1784, Francis Asbury moved the Methodist revival movement into its own denomination – the Methodist Episcopal Church. This had tremendous political impact in Virginia as the Anglican Church had been the officially established state church since the colony's founding charter in 1606.

In 1786, with Americans having just fought a war of independence from the King, the Virginia Assembly was faced with a question. Should Virginia replace the established Anglican Church with the new Episcopal Church, or should they disestablish the concept of an established church altogether? It looked as if the Episcopal Church would be established, being supported by leaders such as George Washington and Patrick Henry.

But Francis Asbury's separation of the Methodist movement into its own denomination meant there would not be enough Episcopal members in the Virginia legislature to vote for that church to be established. Therefore, in 1786, Virginia officially disestablished the Anglican, now Episcopal, Church, thereby allowing all other denominations to be treated equally.

Responding quickly, Britain passed the Consecration of Bishops Abroad Act of 1786 which allowed Anglican Archbishops to consecrate Episcopal Bishops. In 1787, they ordained Episcopal Bishop Samuel Provoost of New York, who was chaplain of the Continental Congress and the first chaplain of the U.S. Senate; and Episcopal Bishop William White of Philadelphia, who served as the second chaplain of the U.S. Senate.

In 1789, Episcopal clergy met in Philadelphia to ratify the initial constitution of the Episcopal Church in America. Nearly one-fourth of all U.S. Presidents were Episcopalian, more than any other denomination, followed by Presbyterian, Methodist and Baptist.

The majority of U.S. Senate Chaplains have been Episcopal (19), followed by Methodist (17), Presbyterian (14), Baptist (6), Unitarian (2), Congregational (1), Lutheran (1), Catholic (1), Seventh–Day Adventist (1).

The 4th Episcopal bishop in America, and the first in Virginia, was Bishop James Madison, cousin of the famous Virginian with the same name, James Madison, the 4th U.S. President.

In recapping, just as the Anglican Church separated from the Catholic Church beginning in 1534, the American Revolution resulted in the Episcopal Church and the Methodist Episcopal Church separating from the Anglican Church.

Other denominations had their own histories of separating from the Anglican Church during the previous two centuries: Presbyterians, Congregationalists, Puritans, Separatists, Pilgrims, Quakers, and Baptists.

Rev. Francis Asbury, one of the first two Methodist Bishops, declared:

• My desire is to live more to God today than yesterday, and to be more holy this day than the last.

• My soul is more at rest from the tempter when I am busily employed.

• We should so work as if we were to be saved by our works; and so rely on Jesus Christ, as if we did no works.

• God is gracious beyond the power of language to describe.

• O what pride, conforming to the world and following its fashions! Warn them, warn them for me, while you have strength and time and be faithful to your duty.

• Preach as if you had seen heaven and its celestial inhabitants, and had hovered over the bottomless pit, and beheld the tortures, and heard the groans of the damned.

Francis Asbury's leadership resulted in the Methodist Church in America growing from just 1,200 people to 214,000, with 700 ordained minsters, by the time of his death in 1816. Asbury befriended Richard Bassett, a signer of the U.S. Constitution. Bassett converted to being a Methodist, freed his slaves, paid them as hired labor and rode joyfully with them to revival meetings.

Shortly after being sworn in as the first President, George Washington was visited in New York on May 19, 1789, by the first two Methodist Bishops in America, Francis Asbury and Thomas Coke. The Bishops greeted Washington with the words:

We ... express to you ... our sincere congratulations, on your appointment to the presidentship of these States. We ... place as full a confidence in your wisdom and integrity, for the preservation of those civil and religious liberties which have been transmitted to us by the Providence of GOD ...

Dependence on the Great Governor of the Universe which you have repeatedly expressed, acknowledging Him the source of every blessing, and particularly of the most excellent Constitution of these States, which is at present the admiration of the world ...

Bishops Asbury and Coke continued:

We enjoy a holy expectation that you will always prove a faithful and impartial patron of genuine, vital religion – the grand end of our creation and present probationary existence ... We promise you our fervent prayers to the Throne of Grace, that GOD Almighty may endue you with all the graces and gifts of his Holy Spirit, that may enable you to fill up your important station to His glory.

On May 29, 1789, President Washington wrote a reply:

To the Bishops of the Methodist–Episcopal Church ... I return to you ... my thanks for the demonstrations of affection and the expressions of joy ... on my late appointment. It shall still be my endeavor ... to contribute ... towards the preservation of the civil and religious liberties of the American people ... I hope, by the assistance of Divine Providence, not altogether to disappoint the confidence which you have been pleased to repose in me ... in acknowledgments of homage to the Great Governor of the Universe ...

Washington continued:

I trust the people of every denomination ... will have every occasion to be convinced that I shall always strive to prove a faithful and impartial patron of genuine, vital religion ... I take in the kindest part the promise you make of presenting your prayers at the Throne of Grace for me, and that I likewise implore the Divine benediction on yourselves and your religious community.

President Calvin Coolidge unveiled an Equestrian Statue of Francis Asbury in Washington, D.C., 1924, stating:

Francis Asbury, the first American Bishop of the Methodist Episcopal Church ... made a tremendous contribution ... Our government rests upon religion. It is from that source that we derive our reverence for truth and justice, for equality and liberty, and for the rights of mankind. Unless the people believe in these principles they cannot believe in our government ... Calling the people to righteousness (was) a direct preparation for self-government. It was for a continuation of this work that Francis Asbury was raised up ...

Coolidge added:

The government of a country never gets ahead of the religion of a country. There is no way by which we can substitute the authority of law for the virtue of man ... Real reforms which society in these days is seeking will come as a result of our religious convictions, or they will not come at all. Peace, justice, humanity, charity – these cannot be legislated into being. They are the result of a Divine Grace ...

He continued:

Frontier mothers must have brought their children to him to receive his blessings! It is more than probable that Nancy Hanks, the mother of Lincoln, had heard him in her youth. Adams and Jefferson must have known him, and Jackson must have seen in him a flaming spirit as unconquerable as his own ... He is entitled to rank as one of the builders of our nation.

On the foundation of a religious civilization which he sought to build, our country has enjoyed greater blessing of liberty and prosperity than was ever before the lot of man.

These cannot continue if we neglect the work which he did.

Coolidge concluded:

We cannot depend on the government to do the work of religion. I do not see how anyone could recount the story of this early Bishop (Asbury) without feeling a renewed faith in our own country.

EARLY BLACK PREACHERS & MISSIONARIES

One of the first black preachers in America was John Marrant. Born a free black in New York in 1755, his father died when he was young. He traveled with his mother to Florida, Georgia and South Carolina. He learned how to read, play the violin and the French horn.

In 1770, as a teenager during the Great Awakening Revival, Marrant was taken to hear evangelist George Whitefield in Charleston, South Carolina, and he came to Christ. Being vocal about his new faith, he was rejected by his family. Marrant wandered away and lived in the woods trusting God to provide. He was befriended by Cherokee and learned their language.

As tensions grew prior to the Revolution, with British inciting Indians, Marrant was arrested by the Cherokee chief and almost executed. Providentially, he preached to the chief, who converted, and gave him complete permission to proclaim the Gospel among the entire tribe. He also preached to the Creek, Catawba and Housaw. John Marrant returned to South Carolina where he preached among slaves.

When the Revolutionary War broke out, he was impressed into the British navy and taken to England where he preached for years. He later returned to preach the Gospel in Nova Scotia to "a great number of Indians and white people" at Green's Harbor near Newfoundland.

The missionary–minded Countess of Huntingdon published *A Narrative of the Lord's Wonderful Dealings with John Marrant, a Black,* which became incredibly popular and went through 17 editions.

In 1750, George Liele was born a slave in Virginia, and taken to Georgia in 1752. When he was 23, he heard Baptist preacher Rev. Matthew Moore and converted. Liele later wrote that he "saw my condemnation in my own heart, and I found no way wherein I could escape the damnation of hell, only through the merits of my dying Lord and Savior Jesus Christ."

George Liele attended the Buckhead Creek Baptist Church, with his master, Henry Sharp, who was a deacon. Henry Sharp encouraged George's preaching and freed him. Liele gained a following and organized them into the congregation of Silver Bluff Baptist Church in Beach Island, South Carolina, 1773, which is considered one of the first black congregations in America.

When the Revolutionary War threatened, George Liele and members of his congregation moved to Savannah, Georgia, where they met in Jonathan Bryan's barn. One of Jonathan Bryan's slaves, Andrew Bryan, converted, was freed, and became the pastor of the congregation — First Bryan Baptist Church — one of the first black Baptist churches in North America.

By 1802, the congregation had grown to 700 members and changed its name to First African Baptist Church. The Savannah Baptist Association wrote on the occasion of his death in 1812 (*Wallbuilder Report*, 2005):

> The Association is sensibly affected by the death of the Rev. Andrew Bryan, a man of color, and pastor of the First Colored Church in Savannah. This son of Africa, after suffering inexpressible persecutions in the cause of his divine Master, was at length permitted to discharge the duties of the ministry among his colored friends in peace and quiet, hundreds of whom, through his instrumentality, were brought to knowledge of the truth "as it is in Jesus."

Another of George Liele's converts was David George. In 1778, when the British captured Savannah during the Revolution, David George went with the British to Nova Scotia, where he founded a black Baptist church, then in 1792, he went with the British to Freetown, Sierra Leon, and started another black Baptist church.

Another early black congregation began in a building on the plantation of Colonel William Byrd III in 1774. It grew into the First Baptist Church of Petersburg, Virginia. (In 1865, the church hosted Virginia's first Republican convention.)

As the Revolutionary War grew more intense, George Liele decided to evacuate. Alan Neely wrote in the *Biographical Dictionary of Christian Missions* (NY: Macmillan, ed. Gerald H. Anderson, 1998, 400–1):

> In order to be evacuated with other royalists and British troops, Liele obtained a

loan and accepted the status of indentured servant to pay the passage for himself, his wife, and his four children on a ship bound for Jamaica. Landing there in January 1783, he soon repaid the debt and secured permission to preach to the slaves on the island.

Thus by the time William Carey — often mistakenly perceived to be the first Baptist missionary — sailed for India in 1793, Liele had worked as a missionary for a decade, supporting himself and his family by farming and by transporting goods with a wagon and team.

Apparently, he never received or accepted remuneration for his ministry, most of which was directed to the slaves. He preached, baptized hundreds, and organized them into congregations governed by a church covenant he adapted to the Jamaican context. By 1814 his efforts had produced, either directly or indirectly, over 8,000 Baptists in Jamaica.

At times he was harassed by the white colonists and by government authorities for "agitating the slaves" and was imprisoned, once for more than three years. While he never openly challenged the system of slavery, he prepared the way for those who did; he well deserves the title "Negro slavery's prophet of deliverance." Liele died in Jamaica.

Lott Cary was born a slave in 1780 near Richmond, Virginia. He heard the Gospel and gave his life to Christ at the age of 27. Joining the First Baptist Church of Richmond, he listened to sermons from the church balcony and was stirred to preach to his own people. He taught himself to read and study the Bible, then was licensed to preach. Working as a craftsman, he saved up enough money to purchase his families' freedom in 1813.

Two years later, at a time of "growing interest in world missions," Cary, with the help of William Crane, founded the Richmond African Missionary Society, working together with the American Baptist Union.

Lott Cary was joined by Colin Teague, also a slave who had purchased his freedom. Teague had become an assistant minister at Richmond's First African Baptist Church.

On January 16, 1821, Lott Cary and Colin Teague set sail on the ship *Nautilus* from Norfolk, Virginia, to Liberia, West Africa. They are considered the first black missionaries from the United States to Africa.

Cary established the first Baptist church in Liberia – Providence Baptist Church of Monrovia. He set up schools and founded the Monrovia Baptist Missionary Society to evangelize local tribes, and served as Liberia's governor in 1828.

George Liele   **Lott Cary**

ↂ

RICHARD ALLEN & THE AME CHURCH
"GOD OUR FATHER, CHRIST OUR REDEEMER, THE HOLY SPIRIT OUR COMFORTER, HUMANKIND OUR FAMILY"

One of the most prominent black preachers was Richard Allen. He was born to slave parents in Philadelphia and sold with his family to a plantation in Dover, Delaware.

As a young man, Richard's master, Stokley Sturgis, gave him permission to attend Methodist religious meetings, where he learned to read.

In the year 1777, at the age of 17, Richard Allen was converted and determined to work even harder to prove that Christianity did not make slaves slothful.

Allen invited Methodist Francis Asbury and other ministers to visit his master and preach to him. Methodists were against slavery, as founder John Wesley had called it "that execrable sum of all villainies."

When Allen's master heard that on the Day of Judgment, slaveholders would be "weighed in the balance and found wanting," he converted and made arrangements for Richard to become free.

Richard Allen became a licensed exhorter, and in 1783, set out preaching in Delaware,

New Jersey, Pennsylvania and Maryland, walking so much that his feet became severely blistered.

In the winter of 1784, Richard Allen, and another black freedman, Harry Hosier, attended the Methodists "Christmas Conference," where the Methodist Church officially separated from the Church of England to form its own denomination.

Allen, together with other black preachers from St. George's Methodist Episcopal Church, began their own church in Philadelphia.

Bishop Francis Asbury preached at the dedication of their first church building, Mother Bethel, in 1794. It is the oldest parcel of real estate in the United States owned continuously by African Americans.

Asbury ordained Richard Allen as the first black deacon in the Methodist Episcopal Church in 1799. Dr. Benjamin Rush and George Washington contributed to Allen's church.

In 1816, Allen led in the forming of an entirely new denomination, the African Methodist Episcopal Church, which was the first African–American denomination organized in the United States.

Jarena Lee became the first woman to receive "authorization" to preach, with Richard Allen giving his approval.

Allen supported AME missionary Rev. Scipio Beanes, who went to Haiti in 1827. Other missionaries went to destinations from San Domingo to Africa. By the date of Richard Allen's death, March 26, 1831, the African Methodist Episcopal Church had grown to over

10,000 members, and since then, to over 3 million.

The motto of the AME Church is: "God Our Father, Christ Our Redeemer, the Holy Spirit Our Comforter, Humankind Our Family."

Richard Allen wrote in his autobiography:

> I was born in the year of our Lord 1760, on February 14th, a slave to Benjamin Chew, of Philadelphia ... My mother and father and four children of us were sold into Delaware State, near Dover, and I was a child and lived with him until I was upwards of twenty years of age, during which time I was awakened and brought to see myself poor, wretched and undone, and without the mercy of God must be lost ...

> I went with my head bowed down for many days. My sins were a heavy burden. I was tempted to believe there was no mercy for me. I cried to the Lord both night and day. One night I thought hell would be my portion. I cried unto Him who delighteth to hear the prayers of a poor sinner; and all of a sudden my dungeon shook, my chains flew off, and glory to God, I cried. My soul was filled. I cried, enough, for me — the Savior died.

Allen stated:

> This land, which we have watered with our tears and our blood, is now our mother country, and we are well satisfied to stay where wisdom abounds and Gospel is free.

CR

"BLACK HARRY" HOSIER – "ONE OF THE BEST PREACHERS IN THE WORLD ... SUCH AMAZING POWER"

Bishop Francis Asbury went to preach in the Southern States. He invited Richard Allen to accompany him, but when he declined, he asked Harry Hosier, who agreed to go.

"Black Harry" Hosier was born in North Carolina. Though he could not read, he carefully listened to Francis Asbury's sermons and memorized them verbatim, along with extensive passages of Scripture.

Hosier later accompanied other Methodist Bishops: Rev. Richard Whatcoat, Rev. Freeborn Garretson, and Rev. Thomas Coke. They let Harry preach at their meetings with great effect. Bishop Thomas Coke described Harry Hosier:

> I really believe he is one of the best preachers in the world. There is such an amazing power that attends his preaching ... and he is one of the humblest creatures I ever saw.

Rev. Henry Boehm wrote (*Wallbuilder Report,* 2005):

> Harry was so illiterate ... that he could not read a word but he could repeat the hymn as if reading it, and quote his text with great accuracy. His voice was musical, his tongue as the pen of a ready writer. He was unboundedly popular, and many would rather hear him than the bishop.

Hosier's sermon "The Barren Fig Tree," preached in 1781, was the first sermon by a black preacher that was copied down and printed. Dr. Benjamin Rush, a signer of the Declaration of Independence, exclaimed that Harry Hosier preached the greatest sermon he had ever heard.

"Black Harry" Hosier became one of the country's most popular preachers, drawing crowds in Virginia, North Carolina, South Carolina, Boston, Connecticut, Philadelphia, Delaware, Baltimore and New York. He was described by historians as: "... a renowned camp meeting exhorter, the most widely known black preacher of his time, and arguably the greatest circuit rider of his day."

Hosier rejected slavery, lifted up the common working man, and charged audiences "that they must be holy." It being too dangerous to preach in the pro–slavery Democrat South, Hosier preached camp meeting revivals along America's western frontier of that era, the territories of Ohio and Indiana.

Hosier's popularity gave birth to "Hoosier" being a term to refer a person of humble, low–born background, who firmly held to fundamental Bible values, as Professor William Pierson of Fisk University explained (*Wallbuilder Report,* 2005):

> Such an etymology would offer Indiana a plausible and worthy first Hoosier –
> "Black Harry" Hoosier – the greatest preacher of his day, a man who rejected slavery
> and stood up for morality and the common man.

CR

"AMAZING GRACE": NEWTON & WILBERFORCE
"BY THE GRACE OF GOD, I AM NOT THE MAN I USED TO BE"

"Amazing grace! How sweet the sound, That saved a wretch like me! I once was lost, but now am found, Was blind, but now I see."

These were the words of John Newton, a former slave ship captain, who died December 21, 1807. At age 11, his mother died and he went to sea with his father. Young John Newton fell in love with Mary Catlett while on shore leave, but overstaying his visit, he missed his ship's departure.

In 1744, he was caught by a "press gang" and dragged onto the ship *HMS Harwich* where he was forced to be a sailor. Newton tried to desert but was caught, stripped to the waist and flogged with 8 dozen lashes. John Newton later wrote:

> Like an unwary sailor who quits his port just before a rising storm, I renounced the hopes and comforts of the Gospel at the very time when every other comfort was about to fail me.

His reckless behavior caused him to be traded to a slave ship. Being a continual problem, Newton was intentionally left on a slave plantation in Sierra Leone, West Africa.

There, the African slave dealer, Amos Clowe, made Newton a slave of his wife, Princess Peye, an African duchess, where he suffered abuse and mistreatment.

Years later, Scottish Missionary David Livingstone mentioned John Newton and the Muslim Arab slave traders' shocking treatment of African slaves (*Missionary Travels and Researches in South Africa,* London, October 1857):

> It was refreshing to get food which could be eaten without producing the unpleasantness described by the Rev. John Newton, of St. Mary's, Woolnoth, London, when obliged to eat the same roots while a slave in the West (Africa).

Livingstone described the Arab slave trade as "a monster brooding over Africa," adding:

> A party of Arabs from Zanzibar were ... at a village in the same latitude as Naliele town ... The Arabs mentioned ... they ... disliked the English, "because they thrash (criticize) them for selling slaves" ... I ventured to tell them that I agreed with the English, that it was better to let the children grow up and comfort their mothers when they became old, than to carry them away and sell them across the sea ...
>
> After many explanations of our abhorrence of slavery, and how displeasing it must be to God to see his children selling one another.

Newton was finally rescued from Africa, but continued his immoral life in the slave trade, deriding Christians with blasphemy that shocked even sailors. Newton wrote in 1778:

> How industrious is Satan served. I was formerly one of his active under–temptors and had my influence been equal to my wishes I would have carried all the human race with me. A common drunkard or profligate is a petty sinner to what I was.

In 1747, Newton was on the slave ship *Greyhound.* The ship was caught in a storm so terrible that he was convinced they would sink. He prayed for the first time in his life. He then read Thomas a Kempis' *Imitation of Christ* and the Bible.

Newton continued in the slave trade for a time, but endeavored to treat slaves humanely. He finally left the slave trade, married Mary Catlett in 1750, and moved to Liverpool, where from 1755 to 1760, he worked as a surveyor of tides. He wrote:

> I am not the man I ought to be, I am not the man I wish to be, and I am not the man I hope to be, but by the grace of God, I am not the man I used to be.

While in Liverpool, Newton met the evangelistic preacher George Whitefield and John Wesley, the founder of Methodism. He was inspired to become a minister and taught himself Greek and Hebrew.

Newton was turned down by the Anglican Archbishop of York, but persisted and was eventually ordained in 1764. He was assigned to the village of Olney, Buckinghamshire, where he humbly proclaimed the saving power of Christ.

In 1767, poet William Cowper moved to Olney, and with his help, Newton composed songs for their weekly prayer meetings. Cowper wrote in the poem "Winter Walk at Noon," 1785: "Nature is but a name for an effect, Whose cause is God."

Newton and Cowper's songs were first published in 1779 in a collection titled "Olney Hymns." The Olney Hymns include: "Oh! for a Closer Walk with God," "God Moves in a Mysterious Way," and "There is a Fountain Filled with Blood," which has the lines:

The dying thief rejoiced to see, That fountain in his day;

And there may I, though vile as he, Wash all my sins away

Wash all my sins away, Wash all my sins away;

And there may I, though vile as he, Wash all my sins away.

The song is a reference to Psalm 51:7 "Wash me, and I shall be whiter than snow"; Rev. 1:5 "Unto Him that loved us, and washed us from our sins in His own blood." It is the understanding that God, being just, has to judge every sin, but God, being love, provided the Lamb to take the judgment for our sins, as prophesied in Isaiah 53:

> The Lord has laid on Him the iniquity of us all. He was oppressed and afflicted, yet He did not open His mouth; He was led like a lamb to the slaughter, and as a sheep before its shearers is silent ... The Lord makes His life an offering for sin ... My righteous servant will justify many, and He will bear their iniquities ... For He bore the sin of many, and made intercession for the transgressors.

John Newton moved to London in 1780 to become rector of St. Mary Woolnoth Church. He continually preached against slavery and published his ghastly experiences in the slave trade in 1788. On a church plaque, and John Newton's tomb, is written:

> John Newton, Clerk, once an infidel and libertine, a servant of slaves in Africa, was, by the rich mercy of our Lord and Savior Jesus Christ, preserved, restored, pardoned, and appointed to preach the faith he had long labored to destroy.

Many influential leaders in England attended John Newton's services.

In 1795, a British member of Parliament, William Wilberforce, came to have a living faith in Jesus Christ through the help of Newton.

Wilberforce initially wanted to become a preacher, but Newton persuaded him to serve God by fighting slavery in the British Parliament, as Britain was the world's largest slave trader in the 19th century.

John Wesley, the same year he died, 1791, wrote a letter to William Wilberforce encouraging him to end slavery. In 1983, President Ronald Reagan wrote in "Abortion and the Conscience of the Nation" (*The Human Life Review*):

> Prayer and action are needed to uphold the sanctity of human life. I believe it will not be possible to accomplish our work of saving lives, "without being a soul of prayer." The famous British member of Parliament William Wilberforce prayed with his small group of influential friends, the "Clapham Sect," for decades to see an end to slavery in the British empire.

Eric Metaxas wrote in his post "BreakPoint: Wilberforce and the "Necessary Evil" (July 26, 2018):

> Historian Christopher D. Hancock wrote, the slave trade "involved thousands of slaves, hundreds of ships, and millions of pounds [sterling]; upon it depended the economies of Britain and much of Europe."
>
> After his dramatic conversion to Jesus Christ in 1785, the heretofore unfocused Wilberforce made three consequential decisions that ended up changing the world:

first, stay in politics, at a time when conventional wisdom held that politics was too dirty a business for Christians; second, work for the abolition of the slave trade in Britain; and, third, work for moral reformation in society.

The movie, *Amazing Grace* (2006) starred Ioan Gruffudd as William Wilberforce and Albert Finney as John Newton. Wilberforce wrote in his journal:

> My walk is a public one ... My business is in the world, and I must mix in the assemblies of men or quit the post which Providence seems to have assigned me.

Wilberforce later added:

> A man who acts from the principles I profess reflects that he is to give an account of his political conduct at the judgment seat of Christ.

Fighting the entrenched, deep–state slavery interests for 11 years, Wilberforce wrote:

> So enormous, so dreadful, so irremediable did the trade's wickedness appear ... that my own mind was completely made up ... Let the consequences be what they would; I from this time determined that I would never rest until I had effected its abolition.

Parliament finally passed an act abolishing the slave trade in 1807, but it took 26 years to abolish slavery throughout the British Empire. Eric Metaxas wrote:

> So it was ... on July 26, 1833, that the Emancipation Act passed its third reading in the House of Commons, ensuring the end of slavery in the British Empire, some three decades before the bloody Civil War would end it in America. When an aged Wilberforce heard the news, he said, "Thank God I have lived to witness [this] Day."

Wilberforce died three days later. President Ronald Reagan wrote:

Wilberforce led that struggle in Parliament, unflaggingly, because he believed in the sanctity of human life. He saw the fulfillment of his impossible dream when Parliament outlawed slavery just before his death.

Considered the most popular Christian hymn ever, John Newton's words began:

Amazing Grace! How sweet the sound
That sav'd a wretch like me!
I once was lost, but now am found,
Was blind, but now I see.

'Twas grace that taught my heart to fear,
And grace my fears reliev'd;
How precious did that grace appear
The hour I first believ'd!

Thro' many dangers, toils, and snares,
I have already come;
'Tis grace hath brought me safe thus far,
And grace will lead me home.

The Lord has promis'd good to me,
His word my hope secures;
He will my shield and portion be
As long as life endures.

Yes, when this flesh and heart shall fail,
And mortal life shall cease;
I shall possess, within the veil,
A life of joy and peace.

The earth shall soon dissolve like snow,
The sun forbear to shine;
But God, who call'd me here below,
Will be forever mine.

CR

SECOND GREAT AWAKENING CAMP MEETINGS–*THE POWER OF REVIVAL INFLUENCES THE MORALITY OF THE PEOPLE*

Thomas Jefferson noted in his *Memorandum Book:*

> I have subscribed to the building of an Episcopalian church, two hundred dollars;
> a Presbyterian church, sixty dollars, and a Baptist church, twenty-five.

On July 14, 1826, the Boston newspaper *Christian Watchman* printed an unverified story that Jefferson dined at Monticello prior to the Revolutionary War with Baptist Pastor Andrew Tribble. The story described how Jefferson inquired of Pastor Tribble how Baptist church government worked, then Jefferson stated that he:

> ... considered it the only form of pure democracy that exists in the world ... It
> would be the best plan of government for the American colonies.

As recorded by Julian P. Boyd in *The Papers of Thomas Jefferson,* Jefferson "organized" a church. He drafted "Subscriptions to Support a Clergyman in Charlottesville," February 1777:

> We the subscribers ... desirous of encouraging and supporting the Calvinistical
> Reformed Church, and of deriving to ourselves, through the ministry of its teachers,
> the benefits of Gospel knowledge and religious improvement ... by regular education
> for explaining the holy scriptures ... Approving highly the political conduct of the

Rev. Charles Clay, who, early rejecting the tyrant and tyranny of Britain, proved his religion genuine by its harmonies with the liberties of mankind ... and, conforming his public prayers to the spirit and the injured rights of his country, ever addressed the God of battles for victory to our arms.

As Virginia's Governor, Jefferson wrote in 1779:

> The reverend Charles Clay has been many years rector of this parish and has been particularly known to me ... In the earliest stage of the present contest with Great Britain while the clergy of the established church in general took the adverse side, or kept aloof from the cause of their country, he took a decided and active part with his countrymen, and has continued to prove ... his attachment to the American cause.

The Calvinistical Reformed Church ceased meeting when subscribers Philip Mazzei and John Harvie moved away, and when Jefferson, depressed after the death of his wife and several children, sailed off to take Ben Franklin's place as the U.S. ambassador to France in 1783.

The religious revival in Virginia continued as part of the "Second Great Awakening." Methodist evangelist Jesse Lee, who traveled a circle of cities, reported in 1787 the "circuits that had the greatest revival of religion" included Albermarle county. Nearly all Baptist and Methodist churches were of mixed races.

In 1788, Rev. John Leland, a friend of Jefferson's and pastor of Goldmine Baptist Church of Louisa, Virginia, personally baptized over 400 people. He wrote in a Resolution for the General Committee of Virginia Baptists meeting in Richmond, Virginia, 1789:

Resolved, that slavery is a violent deprivation of rights of nature and inconsistent with a republican government, and therefore, recommend it to our brethren to make use of every legal measure to extirpate this horrid evil from the land; and pray Almighty God that our honorable legislature may have it in their power to proclaim the great jubilee, consistent with the principles of good policy.

Leland referred to "jubilee" as it was a day in the Hebrew calendar, every fifty years, when all Israelites serving as indentured servants were to be given their freedom.

In 1787, Hampden–Sydney College in Virginia experienced an awakening which spread across the state. In Charlottesville, attorney William Wirt attended the meetings of Presbyterian Rev. James Waddell, who had been influenced by Colonial Preacher Samuel Davies.

Wirt was appointed by President Monroe as U.S. Attorney General, where he defended the rights of Cherokee Indians in *Worcester v. Georgia,* 1832. Wirt wrote of Waddell's preaching:

Every heart in the assembly trembled in unison ... The effect was inconceivable ... The whole house resounded.

In Lee, Massachusetts, Rev. Alvan Hyde reported in 1792:

A marvelous work was begun, and it bore the most decisive marks of being God's work. So great was the excitement, though not yet known abroad, that into whatever section of the town I now went, the people in that immediate neighborhood, would leave their worldly employments, at any hour of the day, and soon fill a large room ... All our religious meetings were very much thronged, and yet were never noisy or irregular ... They were characterized with a stillness and solemnity, which, I believe, have rarely been witnessed ... To the praise of sovereign grace, 1 may add, that the work continued, with great regularity and little abatement, nearly eighteen months.

James Madison, who was a member of St. Thomas Parish where Rev. James Waddell taught, exclaimed of him: "He has spoiled me for all other preaching."

Madison invited Presbyterian preachers to speak at his Montpelier estate, such as Samuel Stanhope Smith and Nathaniel Irwin, of whom he wrote: "Praise is in every man's mouth here for an excellent discourse he this day preached to us."

Methodist Rev. Lorenzo Dow, nicknamed "Crazy Dow," traveled over ten thousand miles preaching to over a million people. His autobiography at one time was the second best-selling book in America, exceeded only by the Bible. Rev. Lorenzo Dow held a preaching camp meeting near Jefferson's home, writing in his *Journal* that on April 17, 1804:

> I spoke in ... Charlottesville near the President's seat in Albermarle County ... to about four thousand people, and one of the President's daughters (Mary Jefferson Eppes) who was present.

In the lawless Kentucky frontier, Rev. James McGready and his small church agreed in 1797:

> Therefore, we bind ourselves to observe the third Saturday of each month for one year as a day of fasting and prayer for the conversion of sinners in Logan County and throughout the world. We also engage to spend one half hour every Saturday evening, beginning at the setting of the sun, and one half hour every Sabbath morning

at the rising of the sun in pleading with God to revive His work.

In June of 1800, 500 members of James McGready's three congregations gathered at the Red River for a "camp meeting" lasting several days, similar to the 18th century Scottish "Holy Fairs," where teams of open–air preachers rotated in a continuous stream of sermons.

On the final day of Rev. James McGready's Red River Camp Meeting: "A mighty effusion of the Spirit" came on everyone "and the floor was soon covered with the slain; their screams for mercy pierced the heavens."

In July of 1800, the congregation planned another camp meeting at the Gaspar River. Surpassing their expectations, 8,000 people arrived, some from over 100 miles away:

> The power of God seemed to shake the whole assembly. Towards the close of the sermon, the cries of the distressed arose almost as loud as his voice. After the congregation was dismissed the solemnity increased, till the greater part of the multitude seemed engaged in the most solemn manner ...
>
> No person seemed to wish to go home–hunger and sleep seemed to affect nobody–eternal things were the vast concern. Here awakening and converting work was to be found in every part of the multitude; and even some things strangely and wonderfully new to me.

On August 7, 1801, though Kentucky's largest city had less than 2,000 people, 25,000 showed up at revival meetings in Cane Ridge, Kentucky. Arriving from as far away as Ohio, Tennessee, and the Indiana Territory, they heard the preaching of Barton W. Stone and other Baptist, Methodist, and Presbyterian ministers. Rev. Moses Hodge described:

Nothing that imagination can paint, can make a stronger impression upon the mind, than one of those scenes. Sinners dropping down on every hand, shrieking, groaning, crying for mercy, convulsed; professors praying, agonizing, fainting, falling down in distress, for sinners or in raptures of joy! ...

As to the work in general there can be no question but it is of God. The subjects of it, for the most part are deeply wounded for their sins, and can give a clear and rational account of their conversion.

A young man who witnessed the Cane Ridge revival wrote in 1802:

The noise was like the roar of Niagara. The vast sea of human beings seemed to be agitated as if by a storm. I counted seven ministers, all preaching at one time, some on stumps, others on wagons ... Some of the people were singing, others praying, some crying for mercy. A peculiarly strange sensation came over me. My heart beat tumultuously, my knees trembled, my lips quivered, and I felt as though I must fall to the ground.

George Addison Baxter, a skeptical professor at Washington Academy in Virginia, published an account of his travels throughout Kentucky, printed in the *Connecticut Evangelical Magazine,* March 1802:

The power with which this revival has spread, and its influence in moralizing the people, are difficult for you to conceive, and more so for me to describe ... I found Kentucky, to appearance, the most moral place I had ever seen. A profane expression was hardly ever heard. A religious awe seemed to pervade the country.

Never in my life have I seen more genuine marks of that humility which ... looks to the Lord Jesus Christ as the only way of acceptance with God ...

I was indeed highly pleased to find that Christ was all and in all in their religion ... and it was truly affecting to hear with what agonizing anxiety awakened sinners inquired for Christ, as the only physician who could give them any help.

Those who call these things "enthusiasm," ought to tell us what they understand by the Spirit of Christianity ... Upon the whole, sir, I think the revival in Kentucky among the most extraordinary that have ever visited the Church of Christ, and all things considered, peculiarly adapted to the circumstances of that country ...

Something of an extraordinary nature seemed necessary to arrest the attention of a giddy people, who were ready to conclude that Christianity was a fable, and futurity a dream. This revival has done it; it has confounded infidelity, awed vice to silence, and brought numbers beyond calculation under serious impressions.

CR

TIMOTHY DWIGHT & THE YALE STUDENT REVIVAL "IT SEEMED FOR A TIME AS IF THE WHOLE MASS OF STUDENTS WOULD PRESS INTO GOD'S KINGDOM"

The Second Great Awakening led to the founding of colleges and universities, such as Lane Theological Seminary (1829) and Oberlin College (1833).

In 1795, Timothy Dwight IV was elected the 8th President of Yale at a time when the students had become largely secular, enamored with French infidelity and the lessening of moral restraints. Soon after his arrival at Yale, Dwight was challenged by seniors to debate whether the Scriptures Old and New Testament were the Word of God.

Dwight listened to their arguments, then systematically demolished them in a series of weekly lectures, giving "a well-reasoned defense of the Bible's accuracy."

Dwight's son, Sereno Edwards Dwight, became U.S. Senate Chaplain in 1816. He wrote *Life of David Brainerd* (1822), and a book about his great-grandfather, *Life and Works of Jonathan Edwards* (ten volumes, 1830). Sereno Edwards Dwight wrote of the Second Great Awakening at Yale:

> From that moment, infidelity was not only without a stronghold, but without a lurking place.

A student related:

> The whole college was shaken. It seemed for a time as if the whole mass of the students would press into the kingdom. It was the Lord's doing, and marvelous in all eyes. Oh, what a blessed change! It was a glorious reformation.

Through the efforts of Timothy Dwight IV, over a third of Yale's student body experienced conversion, with many entering the ministry. A Yale tutor wrote:

> Yale College is a little temple; prayer and praise seem to be the delight of the greater part of the students while those who are still unfeeling are awed with respectful silence.

Spreading to other colleges, hundreds of students entered the ministry and pioneered the foreign missions movement which made a global impact. Young men, along with the first women missionaries, were sent to the American West, and as far away as the Caribbean, Burma and Hawaii.

The Second Great Awakening contributed to the founding of the American Bible Society, the Society for the Promotion of Temperance, the Church of Christ, the Disciples of Christ and the Seventh–Day Adventists.

Christians helped reform prisons, cared for the handicapped and mentally ill, started hospitals, and worked to end slavery with the abolitionist movement.

HAYSTACK PRAYER MEETING & WORLD MISSIONS

"Expect great things from God, Attempt great things for God" was the motto of William Carey, who left England in 1793 to become a missionary to India.

In 1806, during the Second Great Awakening, five Williams College students met by the Hoosic River in Massachusetts near a grove of trees to discuss how to reach the world with the Gospel. Suddenly a thunderstorm poured down torrential rain and the students hid next to a haystack until it passed.

While there, they prayed and committed themselves to world missions. The book *Williamstown and Williams College* by Arthur Latham Perry (1904) recorded:

> The brevity of the shower, the strangeness of the place of refuge, and the peculiarity of their topic of prayer and conference all took hold of their imaginations and their memories.

The Haystack Prayer Meeting led to the founding of the American Board of Commissioners for Foreign Missions, which in the next 50 years sent out 1,250 missionaries to India, China, Hawaii, southeast Asian countries. In 150 years, it sent out 5,000 to mission fields around the world. Missionaries established schools, hospitals and translated the Bible into indigenous languages, even creating written languages.

The first missionary sent out by the American Board of Commissioners for Foreign Missions was Adoniram Judson, born in Massachusetts, August 9, 1788.

At age 16, Judson began attending a college founded in 1764 by Baptist ministers, the College of Rhode Island & Providence Plantations (Brown University).

While there, he became friends with a skeptic and deist student named Jacob Eames. Eames was a fan of the godless French philosophies which emerged after the French Revolution and swept America's college campuses, capturing the minds of impressionable students. Eames convinced Judson to abandon his parent's Christian faith and become a skeptic.

In 1804, after graduating valedictorian of his class at age 19, Judson opened a small school and wrote grammar and math textbooks.

While traveling to New York City in 1808, Judson stayed at a little inn. He was annoyed and not able to get any sleep because the groans of a dying man in a neighboring room kept him awake all night.

Nevertheless, Judson ignored the cries, as his heart had become hardened by his skeptical college friend, Jacob Eames. The next morning, when checking out, Judson inquired of the innkeeper who the man was who had died in the night.

He was petrified when he heard it was none other than Jacob Eames, his college friend. This rude awakening led Adoniram Judson to reaffirm his Christian faith. He would go on to become one of America's first foreign missionaries and the first significant missionary to

Burma – modern day Myanmar.

Adoniram Judson fell in love with Ann Hasseltine. He wrote to Ann's father:

> I have now to ask whether you can consent to part with your daughter early next spring, to see her no more in this world; whether you can consent to her departure for a heathen land, and her subjection to the hardships and sufferings of a missionary life; whether you can consent to her exposure to the dangers of the ocean; to the fatal influence of the southern climate of India; to every kind of want and distress; to degradation, insult, persecution, and perhaps a violent death?

> Can you consent to all this for the sake of Him who left his heavenly home, and died for her and for you; for the sake of perishing immortal souls; for the sake of Zion and the glory of God? Can you consent to all this in hope of soon meeting your daughter in the world of glory, with a crown of righteousness brightened by the acclamations of praise which shall redound to her Savior from heathens saved, through her means, from eternal woe and despair?

At age 23, Adoniram, and his wife Ann, age 22, sailed from New England on February 19, 1812, for Calcutta, India.

Another missionary who sailed with the Judsons was Luther Rice. In India, they all met English Baptist missionary William Carey. The Judsons and Luther Rice switched from Congregationalist to Baptist, which jeopardized their financial support.

They were forced by the British East India Company to leave India. The Judsons sailed for Rangoon, Burma, and Luther Rice returned to America.

Rice dedicated himself to raise money for missions, which led to the establishment of the Southern Baptist Convention. Brown University awarded Rice an honorary doctorate. Rice helped start numerous Baptist seminaries and universities, including The George Washington University in Washington, DC, in 1821, where the main administration building is named Luther Rice Hall.

In Burma, Adoniram and Ann Judson translated Bible Scriptures, preached in Burmese, and started schools.

When war broke out between the British and Burma, Burmese officers burst into the Judson's home. They threw Adoniram on the ground in front of his pregnant wife and tied him up with torture thongs. Accusing him of being a spy for the British, they dragged him away and threw him into the infamous Ava death prison.

After 12 months, Judson was marched with other prisoners, ill and barefoot, to a primitive village near Mandalay. All but one of the other prisoners died.

While Adoniram was in prison, his wife Ann was alone as the only western woman in the entire country. She lived in a tiny shack outside the gate and brought him meager food, as the prison did not feed him. Ann continually lobbied the authorities for his release.

After 20 months of brutal treatment, being in irons and even suspended by his mangled feet, Adoniram was finally released. The British then pressed him into serving as an interpreter between the British and Burmese, where he gained respect from both sides.

Adoniram Judson compiled an *English–Burmese Dictionary* and translated the Bible.

Then, in 1826, Adoniram Judson's wife, Ann, died. Adoniram sank into severe depression. He was later joined by missionaries George Boardman and his wife, Sarah.

It took Judson 12 years to make 18 converts. One of the first was from a man from the Karen people, whom Judson called Ko Tha Byu – "younger brother." He had been a murderer with a diabolical temper, who was captured, and sold into slavery.

Adoniram Judson and George Boardman began witnessing to him, teaching him to read and write. Ko Tha Byu converted to Christianity and was baptized on May 16, 1828. For the rest of his life he was a tireless evangelist to the Karen people.

The Karen people had been a hunted minority scattered in the jungles. Astonishingly, their ancient Karen people beliefs were that there was an all-powerful Creator of heaven and earth who made a man, then took one of the man's ribs and formed a woman.

The Karen people believed that as a result of temptation by a devil, the man and woman fell, but there was a promise that someday a messiah would come to their rescue. The Karen people lived in expectation of a prophecy that white foreigners would bring them a sacred parchment roll instructing them on the way to heaven.

Ko Tha Byu was put into the ministry by Adoniram Judson. With Ko Tha Byu's help, from 1828–1840, membership in the Karen Baptist Church grew to 1,270.

Ko Tha Byu served as the first native Burmese pastor, refounding the church at Rangoon. A mission worker described him: "Ko Tha Byu was an uneducated man; yet he did more good than all of us, for God was with him."

Judson died in April 12, 1850. His life's work resulted in Burma having 100 churches, 123 ministers and over 8,000 baptized Christians. Each July, Baptist churches in Myanmar celebrate "Judson Day." The leader of the Myanmar Evangelical Fellowship stated in 1993:

> Today, there are 6 million Christians in Myanmar, and every one of us trace our spiritual heritage to one man – the Reverend Adoniram Judson.

In the United States, no less than 36 Baptist churches are named after Adoniram Judson, as well as Judson University in Illinois and the town of Judsonia, Arkansas.

His wife, Ann Judson, is the namesake of Judson College in Alabama, as well as a dormitory at Maranatha Baptist University. At Brown University there is a house named after Adoniram Judson, owned by Christian Union.

During World War II, a U.S. Liberty Ship was stationed in the Philippines named the SS Adoniram Judson. Surviving 56 air raid attacks day and night for six days, the ship's captain said "It was miraculous that the bombs did not hit the ship."

Expressing his conviction, Adoniram Judson wrote:

> How do Christians discharge this trust committed to them? They let three fourths of the world sleep the sleep of death, ignorant of the simple truth that a Savior died for them.

☙

INDIANS LOOK FOR "BOOK TO HEAVEN": WHITMANS & NORTHWEST MISSIONS

After the Louisiana Purchase from France in 1803, Jefferson sent Lewis and Clark to explore the Northwest from May 1804 to September 1806, meeting native tribes along the way.

Several years later, in 1831, three Nez Perce Indians and one Flathead Indian, traveled 2,000 miles, all the way from the Oregon Territory to St. Louis, Missouri, looking for the "Book to Heaven."

The Bishop of St. Louis was Rev. Joseph Rosati (1789–1843), who later sent Pierre–Jean De Smet as one of the "Black robe" missionaries to the Indians. Bishop Rosati wrote in the *Annals of the Association of the Propagation of the Faith,* December 31, 1831:

> Some three months ago four Indians who live across the Rocky Mountains near the Columbia River (Clark's Fork of the Columbia) arrived at St. Louis ... After visiting General Clark who, in his celebrated travels, has visited their country ... they came to see our church and appeared to be exceedingly well pleased with it ... Two of our priests visited them ... They made the sign of the Cross and other signs which appeared to have some relation to baptism. The sacrament was administered to them.

A monument of two eagle feathers, standing over eight feet tall, in Calvary Cemetery in St. Louis, Missouri, commemorates the visit of the Indians.

Wyandot Indian chief, William Walker (1800–1874), who had become a Methodist, met the same Indians at the home of territorial governor William Clark, of the Lewis and Clark Expedition (1805–1806). Though modern–day revisionists attempt to discredit the spiritual aspect of the Indians' quest, William Walker, who was the first provisional governor of the Nebraska–Kansas Territory, gave an eye–witness account.

His account was printed, March 1, 1833, in the *Christian Advocate & Journal and Zion's Herald of New York,* a Methodist Episcopal publication which at the time had the largest circulation of any periodical in the world:

> Immediately after we landed in St. Louis, on our way to the west, I proceeded to Gen. Clark's, superintendent of Indian affairs ... While in his office ... he informed me that three chiefs from the Flat–Head nation were in his house, and were quite sick, and that one (the fourth) had died a few days ago.

> They were from the west of the Rocky Mountains ... Curiosity prompted me to step into the adjoining room to see them, having never seen any, but often heard of them. I was struck by their appearance ...

> The distance they had traveled on foot was nearly three thousand miles to see Gen. Clarke, their great father, as they called him, he being the first American officer they ever became acquainted with ...

Walker continued:

Gen. Clark related to me the object of their mission, and, my dear friend, it is impossible for me to describe to you my feelings while listening to his narrative ... (They had heard) the white people away toward the rising of the sun had been put in possession of the true mode of worshiping the great Spirit.

They had a book containing directions how to conduct themselves in order to enjoy his favor and hold converse with him; and with this guide, no one need go astray, but every one that would follow the directions laid down there, could enjoy, in this life, his favor; and after death would be received into the country where the great Spirit resides, and live forever with him ...

Upon receiving this information, they called a national council to take this subject into consideration ... They accordingly deputed four of their chiefs to proceed to St. Louis to see their great father, Gen. Clarke, to inquire of him.

William Walker wrote further of being at William Clark's home in St. Louis, Missouri, in 1831 and meeting the Nez Perce and Flathead Indians:

They arrived at St. Louis, and presented themselves to Gen. Clark the latter was somewhat puzzled being sensible of the responsibility that rested on him; he however proceeded by informing them that what they had been told by the white man in their own country, was true.

Then went into a succinct history of man, from his creation down to the advent of the Savior; explained to them all the moral precepts contained in the Bible, expounded to them the decalogue (ten commandments). Informed them of the advent of the Savior, his life, precepts, his death, resurrection, ascension, and the relation he now stands to man as a mediator – that he will judge the world.

The published account of the Nez Perce and Flathead Indians visiting St. Louis inspired Dr. Marcus Whitman and his wife, Narcissa, to leave Massachusetts and become missionaries to the Indians of Oregon and Washington. Accompanying them were Presbyterian missionaries Henry and Eliza Spalding. This made Narcissa and Eliza the first white women to cross the Rocky Mountains.

In dedicating the Oregon Trail Monument, July 3, 1923, President Warren Harding recounted Dr. Marcus Whitman traveling, clad in buckskin breeches, fur leggings and moccasins,

(An) episode ... took place within these walls ... Seated at his desk ... John Tyler, tenth President of the United States. Facing him ... was the lion–visaged Daniel Webster, Secretary of State.

The door opened and there appeared before the amazed statesmen a strange and astonishing figure. It was that of a man of medium height and sturdy build, deep chested, broad shouldered, yet lithe in movement and soft in step.

He was clad in a coarse fur coat, buckskin breeches, fur leggings, and boot moccasins, looking much worse for the wear ... It was that of a religious enthusiast, tenaciously earnest yet revealing no suggestion of fanaticism, bronzed from exposure to pitiless elements and seamed with deep lines of physical suffering, a rare combination of determination and gentleness – obviously a man of God, but no less a man among men.

Such was Marcus Whitman, the missionary hero of the vast, unsettled, unexplored Oregon country, who had come out of the West to plead that the state should acquire for civilization the empire that the churches were gaining for Christianity ...

Harding continued:

The magnificence of Marcus Whitman's glorious deed has yet to find adequate recognition in any form. Here was a man who, with a single companion, in the dead of winter (1842), struggled through pathless drifts and blinding storms, four thousand miles, with the sole aim to serve his country and his God ...

He was pushing grimly and painfully through this very pass on his way from Walla Walla to Fort Hall, thence, abandoning the established northern route as impassable, off to the South through unknown, untrodden lands, past the Great Salt Lake, to Santa Fe, then hurriedly on to St. Louis and finally, after a few days, again on the home–stretch to his destination, taking as many months as it now takes days to go from Walla Walla to Washington ...

Harding continued:

It was more than a desperate and perilous trip that Marcus Whitman undertook. It was a race against time. Public opinion was rapidly crystallizing into a judgment that the Oregon country was not worth claiming, much less worth fighting for; that, even though it could be acquired against the insistence of Great Britain, it would prove to be a liability rather than an asset ...

Webster ... years before ... had pronounced Oregon "a barren, worthless country, fit only for wild beasts and wild men" ... Whitman ... turning to the President Tyler ... added ... beseechingly: "All I ask is that you will not barter away Oregon or allow English interference until I can lead a band of stalwart American settlers across the plains. For this I shall try to do!" ...

The just and considerate Tyler could not refuse. "Doctor Whitman," he rejoined sympathetically, "your long ride and frozen limbs testify to your courage and your patriotism. Your credentials establish your character. Your request is granted!"

Harding added:

Whitman ... a few months later (1843) ... had completed an organization of eager souls, and led the first movement by wagon train across plains and mountains along this unblazed trail.

What a sight that caravan must have appeared to the roaming savages! And what an experience for the intrepid pioneers! More that two hundred wagons, bearing well-nigh a thousand emigrants, made up the party.

They traveled by substantially the same route that Whitman had taken when he first went out to Oregon; from a rendezvous near what is now Kansas City they moved due northwest across northeast Kansas and southeast Nebraska to the Platte River; followed the Platte to the middle of what is now Wyoming, thence crossing the mountains by way of the Sweetwater Valley and the South Platte; and from Fort Hall, following the well-known route, roughly paralleling the Snake River, into Oregon.

The difficulties of the trip, involving beside the two hundred wagons, the care of women and children, and of considerable herds of livestock, were such that its successful accomplishment seems almost miraculous.

But stern determination triumphed and the result was conclusive. Americans had settled the country ... and in the end the boundary settlement was made on the line of the forty-ninth parallel, your great Northwest was saved, and a veritable Empire was merged in the young Republic.

Never in the history of the world has there been a finer example of civilization following Christianity. The missionaries led under the banner of the cross, and the settlers moved close behind under the star–spangled symbol of the nation.

Harding acknowledged the missionaries by name:

Among all the records of the evangelizing efforts as the forerunner of human advancement, there is none so impressive as this of the early Oregon mission and its marvelous consequences. To the men and women of that early day whose first thought was to carry the gospel to the Indians

–to the Lees, the Spauldings, the Grays, the Walkers, the Leslies, to Fathers De Smet and Blanchet and De Mars, and to all the others of that glorious company who found that in serving God they were also serving their country and their fellowmen

–to them we pay today our tribute; to them we owe a debt of gratitude, which we can never pay, save partially through recognition such as you and I have accorded today.

Unfortunately, when an outbreak of measles occurred, several Cayuse Indians died. The mission was blamed and the Whitmans, along with 11 others, were massacred. President Harding ended his Oregon Trail tribute by acknowledging:

> ... my appreciation both as President of the United States and as one who honestly tries
> to be a Christian soldier, of the signal [distinguished] service of the martyred Whitman.

This highlights a recurring theme in history, namely, the two competing motivations of Greed and the Gospel. Missionaries and virtuous settlers motivated by the Gospel genuinely wanted to be a blessing to native tribes; but opportunistic politicians and settlers motivated by greed wanted to drive tribes off their lands.

Attempting to discern the difference were Chief Moses of the Sinkiuse–Columbia tribe, and Chief Joseph of the Nez Perce tribe. They reluctantly gave up land to avoid war, but in the process, successfully preserved their tribes' existence.

Chief Moses befriended Missionary Henry Spalding and was educated at a Presbyterian mission school. He traveled to Washington, D.C., and met with President Rutherford Hayes.

The unavoidable fact was, that the Northwest was going to be claimed by some power, either by Spain, France, Russia, Britain, or by the United States.

After treaties were negotiated, the Oregon Territory of 286,541 square miles was part of the U.S. becoming: Oregon, Washington, Idaho, parts of Wyoming, and Montana. The State of Washington placed Dr. Marcus Whitman's statue in the U.S. Capitol's Statuary Hall.

CR

JOHN STEWART, MISSIONARY TO WYANDOT INDIANS

In 1786, John Stewart, a free black of mixed race, was born in Powhatten County, Virginia. As a young man, John Stewart learned the blue–dying trade. With his life savings, Stewart started traveling to Tennessee to join his family, but was robbed along the way.

He only made it as far as Marietta, Ohio. Destitute and depressed, John Stewart decided to drink himself to death.

His story is recorded in Joseph Mitchell's book, *The Missionary Pioneer, or A Brief Memoir of the Life, Labours, and Death of John Stewart* (Man of Colour,) Founder, under God of the Mission among the Wyandots at Upper Sandusky, Ohio (New York: printed by J. C. Totten, 1827):

> The loss of his property, the distance from his friends, the idea of poverty and disgrace, together with the wretched situation of his mind on account of his soul's affairs, brought him to shocking determination that he would immediately take measures to hasten his dissolution.

> And for this purpose he forthwith commenced a course of excessive drinking in a public house. This was continued until his nerves became much affected, his hands trembled so it was difficult for him to feed himself.

John Stewart tried to straighten out his life and worked in the country making sugar. Thelma R. Marsh wrote in *Moccasin Trails to the Cross* (United Methodist Church, 1st edition, 1974):

> Stewart ... returned to town, where, contrary to the most solemn vows and promises, which he had previously made to forsake sin and seek the Lord ... An occurrence here took place which much alarmed him: an intimate companion of his was suddenly called by death from time to eternity.

> With this individual he had made an appointment to spend one more night in sin; but death interfered and disappointed them both. Stewart's convictions of mind were thereupon greatly increased, and he began to despair of ever obtaining mercy.

The book, *John Stewart–Missionary Pioneer* (published 1827), stated:

> One day while wandering along the banks of the Ohio, bewailing his wretched and undone condition, the arch enemy of souls suggested to him a remedy, which was to terminate the miseries he endured by leaping into the deep, and thereby putting an end to his existence.

> To this suggestion, he at first felt a disposition to yield, but his attention was arrested by a voice, which he thought called him by name; when on looking around he could see no person, whereupon he desisted from the further prosecution of the desperate project ...

> Then it was that the Lord was pleased to reveal his mercy and pardoning love to his

fainting soul, causing him to burst forth from his closet in raptures of unspeakable joy, declaring what the Lord had done for his poor soul! ...

There being no Baptist church near ... as he walked out one evening he heard the sound of singing and praying proceeding from a house at no great distance. It proved to be a Methodist prayer meeting.

His prejudices at first forbade his going in but curiosity prompted him to venture a little nearer, and at length he resolved to enter and make known his case, which he did.

The book, *John Stewart—Missionary Pioneer* (1827), continued:

Soon after this he attended a Camp Meeting, here he remained for some time with a heavy heart ... He at length resolved ... by taking a place among the mourners of the assembly, where he lay deploring his case all night, even until the break of day, at which time "the sun of righteousness" broke into his dark bewildered soul ...

He heard a sound which much alarmed him: and a voice (as he thought) said to him — "Thou shalt declare my counsel faithfully" at the same time a view seemed to open to him in a Northwest direction, and a strong impression was made on his mind, that he must go out that course into the world to declare the counsel of God ...

He set out without credentials, directions of the way, money or bread, crossed the Muskingum River for the first time, and traveled a northwest course, not knowing whither he went ...

He was frequently informed this would lead him into the Indian country on the Sandusky River, sometimes with, sometimes without a road, without a pilot, without fireworks, sometimes wading the waters and swimming the rivers.

Abraham J. Baughman wrote in *Past and Present of Wyandot County, Ohio: a record of settlement* (Chicago: The S.J. Clark Publishing Company, 1913, Volume 1, page 39–43):

At Pipetown was a considerable body of Delawares ... At this place Stewart stopped, but as the Indians were preparing for a great dance they paid but little attention to him ...

Stewart took out his hymn book and began to sing. He, as is usual with many of his race, had a most melodious voice, and as a result of his effort the Indians present were charmed and awed into perfect silence. When he ceased, Johnny–cake said in broken English, "Sing more."

He then asked if there was any person present who could interpret for him; when old Lyons, who called himself one hundred and sixty years old (for he counted the summer a year and the winter a year) came forward. Stewart talked to them.

John Stewart made it to the tribe of Wyandots, who were called by the French "Huron." They previously had treaties with the French during the French and Indian Wars, 1754–1763, and helped found Detroit. They later made treaties with the British during Revolutionary War and the War of 1812.

John Stewart reached the home of Indian William Walker, Sr., who first believed Stewart to be a run-away slave. Stewart convinced him that he had come to bring the gospel of Jesus Christ to the children of the forest.

Realizing that Stewart could not speak the Wyandot language, William Walker sent him to Jonathan Pointer, a black man who in his youth had been kidnapped by the Wyandots, adopted into their tribe and had learned the Wyandot language.

Pointer served as interpreter for Stewart when he preached, but not wanting his friends to think that he believed, Pointer ended each interpretation with a remark "These are his words, not mine" or "That's what the preacher says, but I don't believe it."

Later, Pointer converted.

One of John Stewart's first Wyandot converts was Chief Between–the–Logs, who years before in a drunken fit killed his wife, only to wake up in horror the next day when he realized what he had done.

Chief Between–the–Logs gave the history:

> Our fathers had religion of their own. They served God and were happy. That was before the White Man came. They worshiped with feasts and sacrifices, dances and rattles. They did what they thought was right. Our parents wished us to do good and they used to make us do good, and would sometimes correct us for doing evil ...
>
> But a great while ago the French sent us a book by the Roman Priest and we listened to him ... We did what he told us ... At last he went away.
>
> Then we returned to our fathers' religion again. But then the Seneca prophet

came and he said that he had talked to the Great Spirit, and he was told what the Indian ought to do.

We listened to him and many followed him. But we found that he told us not to do things and then he did those things himself. So we were deceived ...

Again we took up the religion of our fathers. But then the Shawnee prophet arose. We heard him and some of us followed him for a while, but we had been deceived so often that we watched him very closely, and soon found that he was like all the rest so we left him

Chief Between–the–Logs continued:

Then there was war between our fathers and the President and King George ...

By the time the war was over we were all scattered and many killed and died. Our chiefs thought to get the nation together again. Then the Black Man, Stewart, our brother here (pointed to Stewart) came to us and told us he was sent by the Great Spirit to tell us the true and good way.

But we thought he was like all the rest — that he too wanted to cheat us and get our money and land from us. He told us of our sins and that drinking was ruining us and that the Great Spirit was angry with us. He said that we must leave off these things.

But we treated him ill and gave him little to eat, and trampled on him and were jealous of him for a whole year. Then we attended his meeting in the council house. We could find no fault with him.

The Great Spirit came upon us so that all cried aloud. Some clapped their hands, some ran away, and some were angry. We held our meetings all night, sometimes singing, sometimes praying. By now we were convinced that God had sent him to us. Stewart is a good man.

Eventually, the entire tribe of Wyandot converted to Christianity. In 1821, the Methodist Conference sent Rev. James B. Finley to start the mission school at Upper Sandusky. John Stewart worked with him and taught a Bible class at the Big Springs Reserve.

Rev. James B. Finley recorded the missionary work of *John Stewart with the Wyandots in the History of the Wyandot Mission* (Cincinnati: Methodist Book Concern).

The State of Ohio also published a record of John Stewart's missionary work in *Henry Howe's Historical Collections of Ohio* (published by The Laning Printing Co., Norwalk, OH, 1896, Volume 2).

John Stewart died December 18, 1823, with his last words being: "Be Faithful."

In 1830, a Democrat–controlled Congress hurriedly passed the Indian Removal Act, signed by Democrat President Andrew Jackson, and carried out by Democrat President Martin Van Buren.

The original indigenous Plains tribes were: Wichitas; Apaches; Quapaws; and Caddos.

By the early 1800s, more tribes had arrived: Osages, Pawnees, Kiowas, Comanches, Cheyennes, Arapahos, Delawares, Shawnees, Kickapoos, Chickasaws, and Choctaws.

In 1830, the Indian Removal Act forced over 16,000 to the Oklahoma Indian Territory:

- Cherokee from the Carolinas, Georgia, Tennessee;
- Creek (Muscogee) from Florida, Tennessee, Alabama, Georgia;
- Seminole from Florida;
- Chickasaw from Alabama, Mississippi, Tennessee;
- Choctaw from Alabama, Louisiana, Mississippi, Florida.

Carried out by the Federal Government in the freezing winter, over 4,000 died in what is referred to at the Trail of Tears.

Other tribes were relocated from the Great Lakes, Ohio River Valley, Mississippi River Valley, and eastern states:

Anadarko (Nadaco); Alabama–Quassarte (Koasati); Cahokia; Catawba; Cayuga; Conestoga; Erie; Euchee (Yuchi); Fox; Hainai; Illinois; Iowa; Kaskaskia; Kaw or Kansa; Keechi (Kichai); Keetoowah; Kialegee; Kickapoo; Lipan; Miami; Michigamea; Missouria; Modoc; Moingwena; Nez Perce; Otoe; Ottawa; Omaha; Osage; Pawnee; Peoria; Piankashaw; Ponca; Potawatomi; Sac (Sauk); Seneca; Shawnee; Stockbridge–Munsee; Tamaroa; Tawakoni; Thlopthlocco; Tonkawa; Waco; Wea; Wyandot (Wyandotte)

The Wyandot tribe, in 1843, was the last tribe to leave Ohio. The year before they were removed, English author Charles Dickens traveled through Ohio by stagecoach.

He went from Columbus to Sandusky City, where he boarded a steamer for Buffalo. There, he recorded meeting the Wyandot Indians before they were removed. In his *American*

Notes, Charles Dickens wrote:

> At length ... a few feeble lights appeared in the distance ... an Indian village, where we were to stay until morning ... It is a settlement of Wyandot Indians who inhabit this place. Among the company was a mild old gentleman (Col. John Johnston), who had been for many years employed by the United States government in conducting negotiations with the Indians ...
>
> and who had just concluded a treaty with these people by which they bound themselves, in consideration of a certain annual sum, to remove next year to some land provided for them west of the Mississippi and a little way beyond St. Louis ...

Dickens concluded:

> He gave me a moving account of their strong attachment to the familiar scenes of their infancy, and in particular to the burial places of their kindred, and of their great reluctance to leave them. He had witnessed many such removals, and always with pain.

William Walker, Sr., the Wyandots' principal chief, had been able to secure land on the border between Missouri and Kansas. The Wyandot Indians, brought to Christian faith by the black missionary John Stewart, emigrated west and founded the City of Wyandotte.

The Christian Munsee tribe of Delaware "Lenape" Indians, who were pushed out of New York, New Jersey and Pennsylvania, emigrated there.

Wyandotte City was later renamed Kansas City.

CR

MISSIONARIES TO HAWAII – "OH WHAT A WONDERFUL THING IS THE HAND OF DIVINE PROVIDENCE"

In 1778, British Captain James Cook discovered Hawaii, which he named "The Sandwich Islands" in honor of John Montagu, the 4th Earl of Sandwich — the acting First Lord of the Admiralty.

Captain Cook was killed on his third visit to Hawaii in 1779. When Captain Cook's voyages were read in England, they raised awareness of new lands and inspired a missionary movement, led by William Carey, who took the Gospel to India in 1793.

Henry Opukahai'a was an orphan raised by his uncle to be a pagan priest but he became disillusioned with rituals and chants. He fled Hawaii in 1807 with his friend Thomas Hopu on the American whaling ship Triumph bound for New England.

They were befriended by Christian students at Yale in New Haven, Connecticut, who instructed and prayed with them to become the first Hawaiian Christians in 1815, during the time of the Second Great Awakening.

Henry Opukahai'a studied Greek and Hebrew. He attempted to translate the Book of Genesis and other parts of the Bible into his native tongue, but none of those manuscripts survived.

In his *Memoirs,* which sold 500,000 copies after his death in 1818, Henry Opukahai'a wrote:

> O what a wonderful thing is that the hand of the Divine Providence has brought me from the heathenish darkness where the light of Divine truth never had been. And here I have found the name of the Lord Jesus in the Holy Scriptures, and have read that His blood was shed for many ...

Henry Opukahai'a continued:

> My poor countrymen, without knowledge of the true God, and ignorant of the future world, have no Bible to read, no Sabbath.

Thomas Hopu met General Andrew Jackson, whom he accompanied to New Orleans. Hopu fought the British during the War of 1812, resulting in him being perhaps one of the first Hawaiians to serve in the United States armed forces.

An excellent swimmer, Hopu saved several crewman after a shipwreck. Five times he taken prisoner by the British in the West Indies. Once starving in prison, African slaves gave him food and water, affecting Hopu to forever detest the enslavement of Africans.

The Second Great Awakening in America sparked a global missionary movement. Two years after Henry Opukahai'a's death from typhus, Thomas Hopu went as a missionary with Hiram Bingham and Asa Thurston back to the Hawaiian Sandwich Islands, serving as their translator.

Hiram Bingham's son, of the same name, attended Yale, then returned to spread

Christianity in the Pacific. He was the first to translate the Bible into the language of the people of the Gilbert Islands.

Hiram Bingham's grandson, Hiram Bingham III, discovered the Inca city of Machu Pichu in 1908 and was elected Governor of Connecticut and a U.S. Senator. Hiram Bingham IV was U.S. Vice Consul in France during World War II, where he helped 2,500 Jews escape internment camps of Hitler's National Socialist Workers Party.

The Hawaiian Islands had been united by King Kamehameha I in 1810. In 1819, King Kamehameha I died. His wife, Ka'ahumanu, and his son, Liholiho (King Kamehameha II), abolished the pagan religion with its kapu rules and human sacrifice.

Hiram Bingham and Yale graduate Asa Thurston, with his wife Lucy, were sent to Hawaii by the American Board of Missions on the ship, Thaddeus, arriving at Kailua on March 31, 1820.

They were the first missionaries to Hawaii. The missionaries not only spread Christianity, but confronted drunkenness and vice which had been introduced into the islands by sailors, whalers, and convicts from Botany Bay.

In 1822, Missionaries Hiram Bingham, Asa Thurston, and Elisha Loomis created Hawaii's 12–letter alphabet. They translated the Bible, began a newspaper, set up schools and churches, and convinced the Hawaiian women to wear dresses.

Betsy Stockton, a young African American woman who had been born a slave but was given her freedom, desired to be a Christian missionary. She attended classes at Princeton

Theological Seminary and was commissioned by the American Board of Commissioners for Foreign Missions.

Betsey Stockton was the first single American woman sent overseas as a missionary. On November 22, 1822, she set sail from New Haven, Connecticut, with the second group of missionaries for a five–month voyage to Hawaii.

She set up schools and taught islanders English, Latin, history and algebra. In two years, over 8,000 students attended 200 schools. An edition of Betsey Stockton's Hawaiian diary was published in the *Christian Advocate,* 1824 and 1825, by Dr. Reverend Dr. Ashbel Green, President of Princeton University. Betsey Stockton wrote of an island church service:

> The 29th was the Sabbath. I went in the morning with the family to worship: the scene that presented itself was one that would have done an American's heart good to have witnessed. Our place of worship was nothing but an open place on the beach, with a large tree to shelter us: on the ground a large mat was laid, on which the chief persons sat.
>
> To the right there was a sofa, and a number of chairs; on these the missionaries, the king, and principal persons sat. The kanakas, or lower class of people, sat on the ground in rows; leaving a passage open to the sea, from which the breeze was blowing ...

Betsey continued:

> Mr. R. addressed them from these words, "It is appointed unto all men once to

die, and after death the judgment." Honoru acted as interpreter: the audience all appeared very solemn.

After service the favorite queen called me, and requested that I should take a seat with her on the sofa, which I did, although I could say but few words which she could understand. Soon after, bidding them aloha, I returned with the family ...

Betsey wrote of being the first teacher of Hawaii's first mission school:

In the afternoon we had an English sermon at our house: about fifty were present, and behaved well. In the morning one of the king's boys came to the house, desiring to be instructed in English.

Mr. S. thought it would be well for me to engage in the work at once. Accordingly, I collected a proper number and commenced. I had four English, and six Hawaiian scholars.

In 1823, Queen Ka'ahumanu and six high chiefs requested to be baptized as Christians. She then banned prostitution and drunkenness, resulting in sailors resenting the missionaries' influence. She helped spread the Gospel in the islands, beginning a "Great Awakening."

Queen Ka'ahumanu was presented with the newly completed version of the New Testament in the Hawaiian language just prior to her death.

Her last words were: "I am going where the mansions are ready."

CR

VOLCANO DEFIED & HAWAIIAN GREAT AWAKENING "NO LAW SHALL BE ENACTED WHICH IS AT VARIANCE WITH THE WORD OF THE LORD"

In 1824, the cousin of Kamehameha I, Chiefess Kapiolani, defied the volcano goddess Pele by saying a Christian prayer, climbing down into the lava crater and returning unharmed, then eating the forbidden Ohelo berries.

Chiefess Kapiolani then praised "the one true God," proclaiming:

Jehovah is my God. He kindled these fires. I fear not Pele. All the gods of Hawaii are vain.

The son-in-law of Hiram Bingham was missionary Titus Coans. He gave the account:

Among these converts was the High Priest of the volcano. He was more than six feet high and of a lofty bearing. He had been an idolater, a drunkard, an adulterer, a robber, and a murderer. For their kapas, for a pig or a fowl he had killed men on the road, whenever they hesitated to yield to his demands. But he became penitent, and appeared honest and earnest in seeking the Lord.

His sister was more haughty and stubborn. She was High Priestess of the volcano.

She, too, was tall and majestic in her bearing. For a long time she refused to bow to the claims of the Gospel; but at length she yielded, confessed herself a sinner and under the authority of a higher Power, and with her brother became a docile member of the church.

In 1825, Queen Ke'opuolani was baptized into the Christian faith, speaking Hawaii's Motto, "The Life of the Land is Perpetuated in Righteousness" ("Ua Mau Ke Ea O Ka Aina I Ka Pono").

Titus Coan wrote *Life in Hawaii: An Autobiographical Sketch of Mission Life and Labors, 1835–1881* (NY: Anson D. F. Randolph, 1882, 49–52); and in Michael McClymond's exhaustive work, *Encyclopedia of Religious Revivals in America* (2006):

> I set off Nov. 29, 1836, on a tour around the island ... On reaching the western boundaries of Puna, my labors became more abundant ... They rallied in masses, and were eager to hear the Word.

> Many listened with tears, and after the preaching, when I supposed they would return to their homes and give me rest, they remained and crowded around me so earnestly, that I had no time to eat, and in places where I spent my nights they filled the house to its entire capacity, leaving scores outside who could not enter. All wanted to hear more of the "Word of Life."

> At ten or eleven o'clock I would advise them to go home and to sleep. Some would return, but more remained until midnight. At cock–crowing the house would be

again crowded, with as many more outside.

At one place before I reached the point where I was to spend a Sabbath, there was a line of four villages not more than half a mile apart. Every village begged for a sermon and for personal conversation. Commencing at daylight I preached in three of them before breakfast, at 10 a.m.

When the meeting closed at one village, most of the people ran on to the next, and thus my congregation increased rapidly from hour to hour. Many were "pricked in their hearts" and were inquiring what they should do to be saved. Sunday came and I was now in the most populous part of Puna.

Multitudes came out to hear the Gospel. The blind were led; the maimed, the aged and decrepit, and many invalids were brought on the backs of their friends.

There was great joy and much weeping in the assembly. Two days were spent in this place, and ten sermons preached, while almost all the intervals between the public services were spent in personal conversation with the crowds which pressed around me.

Many of the people who then wept and prayed proved true converts to Christ; most of them have died in the faith, and a few still live as steadfast witnesses to the power of the Gospel.

Soon, native Hawaiian missionaries began evangelizing The Marquesas Islands, Polynesia, and other Pacific Islands.

When Liholiho (King Kamehameha II) died, his brother, King Kamehameha III, ascended to the throne, having the longest reign in Hawaii's history, 1825–1854.

The various island kingdoms of the Pacific had no navies capable of repelling the global maritime powers of the day, namely, Portuguese, Spanish, Dutch, French, British, and Japanese. King Kamehameha III was instrumental in using diplomacy to keep the Kingdom of Hawaii from being taken over by the British and French.

King Kamehameha III introduced the first Hawaiian Constitution in 1840:

> Kingdom of Hawaii Constitution of 1840, Declaration of Rights of People and Chiefs:
>
> God hath made of one blood all nations of men to dwell on the earth," in unity and blessedness. God has also bestowed certain rights alike on all men and all chiefs, and all people of all lands ...
>
> God has also established government, and rule for the purpose of peace ... We are aware that we cannot ourselves alone accomplish such an object — God must be our aid, for it is His province alone to give perfect protection and prosperity. —
>
> Wherefore we first present our supplication to HIM, that He will guide us to right measures and sustain us in our work ...

Hawaii's 1840 Constitution continued:

> It is therefore our fixed decree, I. That no law shall be enacted which is at variance with the word of the Lord Jehovah, or at variance with the general spirit of His word. All laws of the Islands shall be in consistency with the general spirit of God's law.

II. All men of every religion shall be protected in worshiping Jehovah, and serving Him, according to their own understanding, but no man shall ever be punished for neglect of God unless he injures his neighbor, or brings evil on the kingdom ...

The above constitution has been agreed to by the Nobles, and we have hereunto subscribed our names, this eighth day of October, in the year of our Lord 1840, at Honolulu, Oahu. (Signed) Kamehameha III. Kekauluohi.

King Kamehameha III granted the "Ka Wai" freshwater springs where High Chiefess Ha'o frequented to be the location for building of the historic Kawaiaha'o Church.

Located on the Island of O'ahu, the Kawaiaha'o Church is listed on the state and national registers of historic sites, as it is one of the first Christian churches in Hawaii. Built between 1836–1842 in New England style architecture, Kawaiaha'o Church was called the "Westminster Abbey of Hawaii."

Constructed with 14,000 coral slabs, quarried by hand from reefs 10 to 20 feet under water – each slab weighed more than 1,000 pounds. Within its walls the kingdom's royalty prayed, sang hymns, were married, christened their children, and finally laid in state. On the grounds surrounding the church are buried some of the original missionaries.

Hawaii became a U.S. Territory July 7, 1898, when President McKinley signed the Treaty of Annexation. In 1959, Hawaii became the 50th U.S. State. The occasion was marked by ceremonies within the sanctuary walls of the Kawaiaha'o Church.

❧

CHARLES FINNEY'S REVIVAL "EVERY MEMBER MUST WORK" – "CHRISTIANS MUST VOTE FOR HONEST MEN ... INSTEAD OF VOTING FOR A MAN BECAUSE HE BELONGS TO THEIR PARTY"

*W*illiam *Blackstone's Commentaries* on the Laws of England profoundly influenced America. Blackstone wrote:

The Creator is a Being, not only of infinite power, and wisdom, but also of infinite goodness ...

Every man now finds ... his reason is corrupt, and his understanding full of ignorance and error ... This has given manifold occasion for the benign interposition of Divine Providence; which, in ... the blindness of human reason, hath been pleased ... to discover ... its laws by an immediate and direct revelation. The doctrines thus delivered we call the revealed or divine law, and they are to be found only in the Holy Scriptures.

Blackstone's Commentaries was studied by John Adams and Thomas Jefferson, as well as Abraham Lincoln. While running a General Store in New Salem, Illinois, in 1831, Abraham Lincoln narrated:

One day a man who was migrating to the West drove up in front of my store with a wagon which contained his family and household plunder. He asked me if I would buy an old barrel for which he had no room in his wagon, and which he said contained nothing of special value.

I did not want it, but to oblige him I bought it, and paid him, I think, half a dollar for it. Without further examination I put it away in the store and forgot all about it ...

Sometime after, in overhauling things, I came upon the barrel, and emptying it upon the floor to see what it contained, I found at the bottom of the rubbish a complete edition of *Blackstone's "Commentaries."*

I began to read those famous works, and I had plenty of time; for during the long summer days, when the farmers were busy with their crops, my customers were few and far between ... The more I read, the more intensely interested I became. Never in my whole life was my mind so thoroughly absorbed. I read until I devoured them.

In the early 1800s, all one had to do to become a lawyer was to study founding documents and law books, such as *Blackstone's Commentaries,* apprentice with an attorney, and sit before a bar exam.

Blackstone's Commentaries also influenced a young attorney, 29-year-old Charles Finney. He saw so many references to Bible verses in it that he bought a Bible and began reading it.

On October 10, 1821, Charles Finney decided to head into the woods near his home and pray to the God of the Bible, saying: "I will give my heart to God, or I never will come down from here." After several hours, he returned to his office, dramatically touched. He later wrote:

> The Holy Spirit ... seemed to go through me, body and soul ... Indeed it seemed to come in waves of liquid love, for I could not express it in any other way.

The next morning, at his law office, a church deacon suing a fellow–church member asked Finney about his case. Finney replied: "I have a retainer from the Lord Jesus Christ to plead his cause, and cannot plead yours."

Finney began presenting the Gospel with a convincing lawyer's argument. He would also pray using common, colloquial language rather than the formal, traditional King's English. He began the tradition of an "altar call" in his 1830 revival in Rochester, New York:

> I had found, that with the higher classes especially, the greatest obstacle to be overcome was their fear of being known as anxious inquirers. They were too proud ...

> Something was needed, to make the impression on them that they were expected at once to give up their hearts; something that would call them to act, and act as publicly before the world, as they had in their sins; something that would commit them publicly to the service of Christ ...

> I had called them simply to stand up in the public congregations ... to bring them out from among the mass of the ungodly, to a public renunciation of their sinful ways, and a public committal of themselves to God.

Finney's revival preaching paved the way for evangelists Dwight L. Moody, Billy Sunday and Billy Graham.

Charles Finney's 1835 *Lectures on Revivals of Religion* inspired George Williams to found the YMCA–Young Men's Christian Association in 1844. Finney's sermons inspired William and Catherine Booth to found what would be called The Salvation Army in 1865.

Charles Finney formed the Benevolent Empire, a network of volunteer organizations to aid poor and aged with healthcare and social needs, which in 1834 had a budget rivaling the Federal Government.

Back then, there was no government run welfare programs. It was the churches and volunteer organizations that took care of the sick and poor.

Finney organized the Broadway Tabernacle in New York in 1831. Concerning the Kingdom of God, he wrote: "Every member must work or quit. No honorary members."

This revival motivated Christians to show the love of Christ to the world through actions, such as founding hospitals, orphanages, homes for the aged, missionary societies, and caring for the poor.

Finney's preaching also led to the formation of abolitionist societies to end slavery. During Finney's term as president of Oberlin College, 1851–1866, the school served as a station on the Underground Railroad, smuggling slaves to freedom. Under Finney's leadership, Oberlin College granted the first college degree in the United States to a black woman, Mary Jane Patterson.

After Finney's death, August 16, 1875, some began preaching a "social gospel" which only emphasized works and progressive change but neglected to evangelize. This movement, at length, became divorced from the motivation to bring people to a saving faith in Jesus.

This offshoot morphed into "social justice" and "liberation theology" groups. Some of these groups use tactics of agitation, division, community organizing, and violence to achieve their goals, breaking commandments not to covet or steal, sowing discord in a way which Jesus would have condemned.

Insisting Christians stay focused on the Gospel's main purpose of reconciling men and women to God through the cross of Jesus, Charles Finney wrote in his article, "The Decay of Conscience" (*The Independent of New York*, December 4, 1873):

> Christ crucified for the sins of the world is the Christ that the people need. Let us rid ourselves ... of neglecting to preach the law of God until the consciences of men are asleep. Such a collapse of conscience in this land could never have existed if the Puritan element in our preaching had not in great measure fallen out ...

He continued:

> If immorality prevails in the land, the fault is ours in a great degree. If there is a decay of conscience, the pulpit is responsible for it.

> If the public press lacks moral discrimination, the pulpit is responsible for it. If the church is degenerate and worldly, the pulpit is responsible for it.

> If the world loses its interest in religion, the pulpit is responsible for it. If Satan

rules in our halls of legislation, the pulpit is responsible for it.

If our politics become so corrupt that the very foundations of our government are ready to fall away, the pulpit is responsible for it.

Let us not ignore this fact, my dear brethren; but let us lay it to heart, and be thoroughly awake to our responsibility in respect to the morals of this nation.

Finney's insistence on leaders having virtue and backbone was an effort to counteract weak-willed and immoral politicians who were easily compromised by intimidation and manipulation. Finney gave the antidote to the selfish motivations of corrupt politicians in Lecture XV "Hindrances to Revival" (*Revival Lectures,* 1855):

The church must take right ground in regard to politics. Do not suppose, now, that I am going to preach a political sermon, or that I wish to have you join and get up a Christian party in politics.

No, I do not believe in that. But the time has come that Christians must vote for honest men, and take consistent ground in politics, or the Lord will curse them ...

Finney continued:

They must be honest men themselves, and instead of voting for a man because he belongs to their party, Bank or Anti–Bank, Jackson, or Anti–Jackson, they must find out whether he is honest and upright, and fit to be trusted.

They must let the world see that the church will uphold no man in office, who is known to be a knave, or an adulterer, or a Sabbath–breaker, or a gambler ...

Every man can know for whom he gives his vote. And if he will give his vote only for honest men, the country will be obliged to have upright rulers ...

He stated further:

The church must act right or the country will be ruined. God cannot sustain this free and blessed country, which we love and pray for, unless the church will take right ground.

Politics are a part of religion in such a country as this, and Christians must do their duty to the country as a part of their duty to God.

It seems sometimes as if the foundations of the nation were becoming rotten, and Christians seem to act as if they thought God did not see what they do in politics. But I tell you, He does see it, and He will bless or curse this nation, according to the course they take.

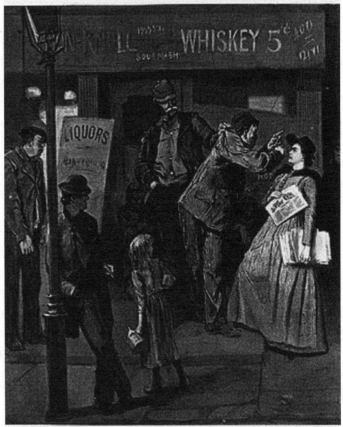

CR

WILLIAM & CATHERINE BOOTH: THE SALVATION ARMY – MINISTERED TO THE POOR, DRUNK, OUTCAST, WHILE FIGHTING SEX–TRAFFICKING

Millions of poor, destitute, and hungry in 128 countries are helped in their "physical and spiritual needs" through homeless shelters, charity shops, disaster relief and humanitarian aid provided by The Salvation Army.

The Salvation Army was founded by William Booth, who was born April 10, 1829.

At the age of 13, Booth was sent to apprentice as a pawnbroker. His job made him aware of poverty, and the humiliation and degradation poor people suffered.

Becoming a Christian as a teenager, Booth studied the writings of America's Second Great Awakening preacher Charles G. Finney, particularly on the subject of revival. This led Booth to begin boldly sharing his faith with others.

William Booth, at the age of 26, married Catherine Mumford in 1855, and together they founded The Christian Mission to minister to the poor, drunk, outcast, and wretched of the dirty and dangerous streets of London's East End slums.

They fought to end child sex–trafficking and teenage prostitution in England. Catherine

Booth said:

> I felt as though I must go and walk the streets and besiege the dens where these hellish iniquities are going on. To keep quiet seemed like being a traitor to humanity.

The Booths helped expose a child prostitution ring that took advantage of poor families by buying their young girls with the false promise of a giving them a better future, but instead sold them to brothels throughout Europe.

The Booths arranged to buy a girl out of this trade in order to expose it, but those profiting from the prostitution ring entangled the Booths in a much publicized trial. They were eventually absolved of all charges, and the corresponding national publicity increased their support to end the evil trade.

With the help of Josephine Butler, The Salvation Army worked to pass England's Criminal Law Amendment Act in 1885, raising the age of consent for sex to adulthood, whereas before it was only at 13 years of age.

In 1884, The Salvation Army established the first rescue home in London for women and girls escaping sex trafficking and prostitution. In 30 years, the number of Salvation Army rescue homes grew from one in Whitechapel to 117 homes around the world.

Adopting uniforms and a semi–military system of leadership, The Salvation Army ministered to the poor, drunk and outcast, while fighting sex–trafficking and teenage prostitution. William Booth wrote:

> While women weep, as they do now, I'll fight; while little children go hungry, I'll

fight; while men go to prison, in and out, in and out, as they do now, I'll fight– while there is a drunkard left, while there is a poor lost girl upon the streets, where there remains one dark soul without the light of God—I'll fight! I'll fight to the very end!

Beginning in 1880, Catherine Booth grew concerned over "sweat labor" shops where women and children worked long hours in very poor conditions, particularly in match making factories where white phosphorous was used.

Exposure to white phosphorus caused one's skin to yellow, hair to fall out, and phossy jaw, where the jaw glowed a greenish–white color, then turned black and rotted away, leading to death. The Booths' efforts led to the adoption of safer matches which were struck on sandpaper. William Booth said:

> We must wake ourselves up! Or somebody else will take our place, and bear our cross, and thereby rob us of our crown.

By the year 1879, The Salvation Army had grown to 81 mission stations staffed by 127 full-time evangelists with over 1,900 voluntary speakers holding 75,000 meetings a year.

William Booth was awarded an honorary degree from Oxford. He met King Edward VII at Buckingham Palace, Winston Churchill, and was awarded the Badge of Honor on behalf of the city of London.

In 1880, The Salvation Army opened work in the United States, followed by missions in over 100 countries, including: France, Australia, India, Switzerland, Sweden, Canada, South Africa, New Zealand, Jamaica, Hong Kong and mainland China.

On March 28, 1885, The Salvation Army was officially organized in the United States. William Booth personally traveled to America, where he met President Theodore Roosevelt. He later sent President Roosevelt a telegram, March 7, 1903:

> I am more than impressed with the greatness of the Nation at whose head you have been placed by the Providence of God. I pray that He may spare you all the wisdom needed ...

> These kindly feelings which you are known to entertain towards those who grow in misery and helplessness even in this greatly favored country ... May the blessing of Him that maketh rich and addeth no sorrow be on the White House and the Nation it represents.

William Booth opened a session of the United States Senate with prayer. The editor of *The Salvation Army's Conqueror* magazine, Major T.C. Marshall, sent a letter to Booker T. Washington, founder of the Tuskegee Institute, thanking him for his favorable comments regarding The Salvation Army's effort to minister to poor blacks in America's South.

Booker T. Washington replied, July 28, 1896:

> I am very glad to hear that The Salvation Army is going to undertake work among my people in the southern states. I have always had the greatest respect for the work of The Salvation Army especially because I have noted that it draws no color line in religion ...

> In reaching the neglected and, I might say, outcasts of our people, I feel that

your methods and work have peculiar value ... God bless you in all your unselfish Christian work for our country.

William Booth stated:

The chief danger of the 20th century will be religion without the Holy Ghost, Christianity without Christ, forgiveness without repentance, salvation without regeneration, politics without God, and Heaven without Hell.

Growing blind, William Booth finally died in 1912. Over 150,000 people viewed his casket with 40,000 attending his funeral, including the Queen of England.

In 1904, Booth's daughter, Evangeline, became the Commander of The Salvation Army's United States forces. Under her leadership, The Salvation Army not only evangelized, but organized programs for unwed mothers, the homeless and disaster relief, especially after the 1906 San Francisco earthquake and in U.S. Army canteens during World War I.

In appreciation for The Salvation Army's work during the war, Evangeline Booth was awarded the Distinguished Service Medal by President Woodrow Wilson in 1919.

The New York Times published an article on August 07, 1927, titled:

FAR–FLUNG ACTIVITY OF SALVATION ARMY; Wherever One Goes in New York It Is to Be Found "Just Around the Corner." IT HAS 47 INSTITUTIONS These Range Through Training Schools to Hospitals, Nurseries, Refuges and Homes.

When Evangeline became International Commander-in-Chief of The Salvation Army, she received a telegram from President Franklin D. Roosevelt, September 4, 1934, saying:

Please accept my sincere congratulations on your election as General of The Salvation Army throughout the world.

In these troubled times it is particularly important that the leadership of all good forces shall work for the amelioration of human suffering and for the preservation of the highest spiritual ideals ...

Your efforts as Commander-in-Chief of The Salvation Army ... have earned the gratitude and admiration of millions of your countrymen.

On December 1, 1965, President Lyndon Johnson remarked to The Salvation Army in New York:

For a century now, The Salvation Army has offered food to the hungry and shelter to the homeless — in clinics and children's homes, through disaster relief, in prison and welfare work, and a thousand other endeavors.

In that century you have proved time and again the power of a handshake, a meal, and a song. But you have not stopped there. You have demonstrated also the power of a great idea.

President Lyndon Johnson continued:

The voice of The Salvation Army has reminded men that physical well-being is just not enough; that spiritual rebirth is the most pressing need of our time and of every time; that the world cannot be changed unless men change.

That voice has been clear and courageous–and it has been heard. Even when other armies have disbanded, I hope that this one will still be on the firing line.

Ronald Reagan stated:

The Salvation Army embodies compassion and Christian love in feeding the hungry, caring for the homeless, and attending to the afflicted and downtrodden.

William Booth is credited with saying:

Most Christian organizations would like to send their workers to Bible college for five years. I would like to send our workers to Hell for five minutes. That would prepare them for a lifetime of compassionate ministry.

The Salvation Army faithfully followed in the steps of William Booth, who wrote:

What are you living for? What is the deep secret purpose that controls and fashions your existence? What do you eat and drink for? What is the end of your marrying and giving in marriage – your money-making and toilings and plannings? Is it the salvation of souls, the overthrow of the kingdom of evil, and the setting up of the Kingdom of God?

If not, you may be religious ... but I don't see how you can be a Christian.

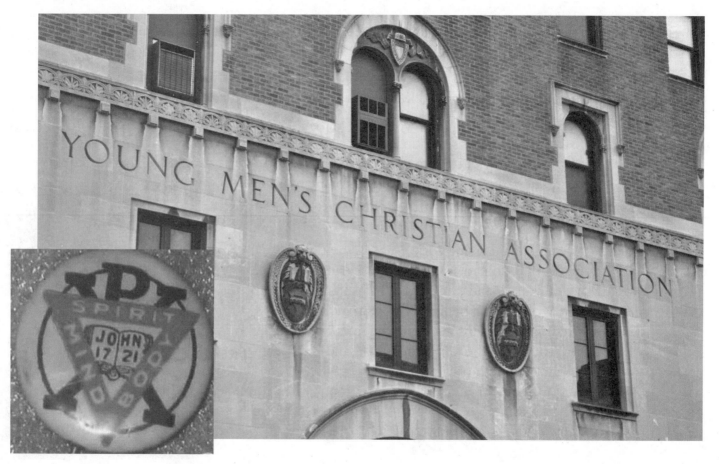

CR

GEORGE WILLIAMS & THE YMCA – "THE ONLY POWER IN THE WORLD THAT CAN KEEP ONE FROM SIN IS ... THE KNOWLEDGE OF THE LORD JESUS AS A PRESENT SAVIOR"

The U.S. Census Bureau statistics (2009) report that over 24 million Americans play BASKETBALL and over 10 million Americans play VOLLEYBALL.

Did you know basketball and volleyball were invented by instructors at the Young Men's Christian Association – YMCA!

James Naismith, a medical doctor and Presbyterian minister, invented the game of basketball at the YMCA training school in Springfield, Massachusetts, in 1891.

His colleague, William Morgan, was the physical education director at the YMCA in Holyoke, Massachusetts. Morgan invented the sport of volleyball in 1895.

Charles Finney's 1835 *Revival Lectures* inspired George Williams to found the YMCA–Young Men's Christian Association in 1844. Williams, who died November 6, 1905, stated:

> My life-long experience as a business man, and as a Christian worker among young
> men, has taught me that the only power in this world that can effectually keep one
> from sin, in all the varied and often attractive forms ... is that which comes from an

intimate knowledge of the Lord Jesus Christ as a present Savior ...

George Williams continued:

> And I can also heartily testify that the safe Guide–Book by which one may be led to Christ is the Bible, the Word of God, which is inspired by the Holy Ghost.

The Young Men's Christian Association has grown to a membership of millions in 124 countries. The early 1881 emblem for the YMCA had the names of the five parts of the world: Europe, Asia, Oceania, Africa and America.

At the center of the emblem was an open Bible displaying John 17:21, referencing the verse: "That they all may be one; as thou, Father, art in me, and I in thee, that they also may be one in us: that the world may believe that thou hast sent me." In 1885, the words "Spirit–Mind–Body" in a triangle were added. Underneath the triangle were the letters XP, called the "Chi–Rho," which were the first two Greek letters of the name of Christ.

In Switzerland, the Geneva chapter of the YMCA was founded by Henri Dunant in 1852. As quoted in Martin Gumpert's book *Dunant, The Story of the Red Cross* (NY: Oxford University Press, 1938, p. 22), Henri Dunant stated:

> A group of Christian young men has met together in Geneva to do reverence and worship to the Lord Jesus whom they wish to serve ... They have heard that among you, too, there are brothers in Christ, young like themselves, who love their Redeemer and gather together that under His guidance, and through the reading of the Holy Scriptures, they may instruct themselves further. Being deeply edified thereby, they wish to unite with you in Christian friendship.

In 1859, Henri Dunant organized care for 23,000 dying and wounded at the Battle of Solferino, Italy. Henri Dunant then founded of the International Red Cross in 1863, for which he became the first recipient of the Nobel Peace Prize.

In 1876, when Turkey was at war with Russia, the Red Cross introduced the name Red Crescent to allow Christian–motivated charity and humanitarian work to be carried on in Islamic countries.

In 1897, Henri Dunant supported Jews in their effort to repopulate their traditional homeland by being one of the few non-Jews to attend the First Zionist Congress in Basel.

During the Civil War, D.L. Moody ministered to soldiers on the battle–lines with the YMCA's United States Christian Commission.

When the 1871 Great Chicago Fire destroyed Chicago's YMCA, D.L. Moody raised funds to rebuild it. Chicago White Stocking baseball star Billy Sunday began attending YMCA meetings in 1886 before beginning his career as a revival preacher.

Booker T. Washington's Tuskegee Institute began a Bible Training school in 1893 to prepare students for Christian ministry. Students helped out at community churches on Sundays; staffed a Humane Society; cared for area sick and needy; and ran a YMCA.

In *Up From Slavery* (1901), he wrote:

> While a great deal of stress is laid upon the industrial side of the work at Tuskegee, we do not neglect or overlook in any degree the religious and spiritual side. The school is strictly undenominational, but it is thoroughly Christian, and the spiritual

training of the students is not neglected. Our preaching service, prayer–meetings, Sunday–school, Christian Endeavor Society, Young Men's Christian Association, and various missionary organizations, testify to this.

Booker T. Washington spoke at Memorial Hall in Columbus, Ohio, May 24, 1900, as described in *The Booker T. Washington Papers,* Vol. 5: 1899–1900 (University of Illinois Press, ed. Louis R. Harlan and Raymond W. Smock, 1976, p. 543–544):

> Dr. Washington began his address after a quartet sang. He spoke of the 91 YMCA Organizations for colored youths; of the 5,000 colored men studying the Bible, and of the 640 Bible students at Tuskegee.

The President of the student YMCA chapter at Cornell University was John R. Mott. He went on to serve as General Secretary of the International YMCA Committee. For his efforts during World War I, John Mott was awarded the Nobel Peace Prize in 1946.

John R. Mott stated:

> I have a hard fight before me in crushing self but it must and will be done. I shall be wholly consecrated and strive to be like Christ.

On October 24, 1914, President Woodrow Wilson addressed the 70th anniversary of the YMCA:

> Christ came into the world to save others, not to save himself; and no man is a true Christian who does not think constantly of how he can lift his brother.

Wilson continued:

I do believe that at 70 the YMCA is just reaching its majority. A dream greater even than George Williams ever dreamed will be realized in the great accumulating momentum of Christian men throughout the world ... These 70 years have just been a running start ... now there will be a great rush of Christian principle upon the strongholds of evil and of wrong in the world. Those strongholds are not as strong as they look ... All you have to do is to fight, not with cannon but with light ... That, in my judgment, is what the Young Men's Christian Association can do ...

President Wilson concluded:

Eternal vigilance is the price, not only of liberty, but of a great many other things ... It is the price of one's own soul ... What shall he give in exchange for his own soul, or any other man's soul? ... There is a text in Scripture ... It says godliness is profitable in this life as well as in the life that is to come ...

This world is intended as the place in which we shall show that we know how to grow in the stature of manliness and of righteousness. I have come here to bid Godspeed to the great work of the Young Men's Christian Association.

In June of 1942, during World War II, the YMCA printed and distributed prayer books to U.S. soldiers and sailors:

The New Testament–An American Translation – Special Edition published for the Army and Navy Department by The National Board of the Young Men's Christian Associations – One of the Agencies of the United States Service Organization – Association Press, 247 Madison Avenue, New York.

George Williams and the YMCA inspired a prominent woman in England, Mary Jane Kinnaird, to found the Young Women's Christian Association in 1855.

Kinnaird worked with Florence Nightingale to train nurses to care for soldiers during the Crimean War with Russia. She led a prayer movement for world evangelism, as recorded in Donald Fraser's book *Mary Jane Kinnaird* (London: Nisbet & Co., 1890). She wrote in a tract that believers should offer: "united prayer in reference ... to the condition of the Jews, Mohammedans, and the heathen world."

Mary Jane Kinnaird continued:

> Prayer ... awakens such strong opposition ... from the world, the flesh, and the devil ... Hence the power of prayer — when to one God and Father, through one Lord and Savior Jesus Christ, and by one Holy Spirit, the prompter of prayer, the multitude of them that believe appeal for ... strength to fight the good fight of faith.

Another organization inspired by Christian charity was Goodwill Industries, founded in 1902 by United Methodist minister Rev. Edgar James Helms. As recorded in *Pioneering in Modern City Missions* (Boston, MA: Morgan Memorial Printing Dept., 1927, chp. III, *The Relation of the Church to Industrial Evangelism,* p. 126–7), Rev. E.J. Helms challenged at the Council of Cities, Baltimore, MD., April 26, 1918:

> If the spirit of God is to dominate the whole social order, then must He be manifest as much in the family and industry and state as He is in the Church. The Church has a greater task of evangelism than to secure individuals who will lift their hands for prayer or sign a card or shake hands with an evangelist ...

Helms continued:

Employer and employee must shake hands in mutual respect and cooperation. The era of exploitation and competition between nations and races must end in mutual helpfulness and goodwill. Jesus Christ and His Gospel must permeate industry and every human interest as well as preaching and education. The Church is His divinely appointed agency for this task.

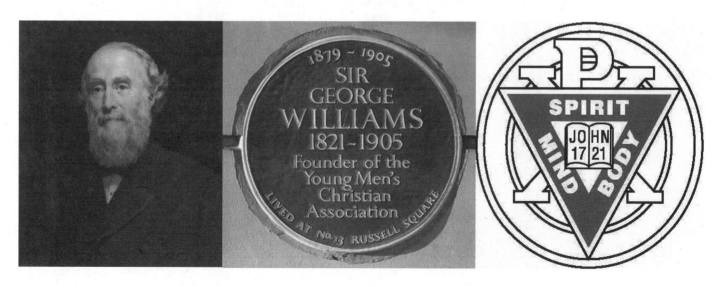

CR

THOUSANDS JOIN LAYMAN'S PRAYER REVIVAL & THIRD GREAT AWAKENING – RESULTING IN MORAL REFORM

In 1844, a New England farmer named William Miller sparked national attention by predicting Christ would return on October 22, 1844. The Millerites' Great Disappointment caused many to abandon their faith.

The nation also experienced the Mexican–America War, 1846–1848, and the California Gold Rush in 1849. A cholera epidemic swept the nation, killing 150,000 and only ended after President Zachary Taylor proclaimed a day of fasting.

Rising to the national forefront was the issue of slavery. In 1850, the Fugitive Slave Law and the Compromise of 1850 were passed, which instead of defusing the conflict of slavery, intensified it.

In 1851, Harriet Beecher Stowe published the anti-slavery novel *Uncle Tom's Cabin*. In 1854, Democrat Senator from Illinois Stephen Douglas pushed through the Kansas–Nebraska Act, after which a flood of pro-slavery Democrats went west, causing the conflict called "bleeding Kansas."

In 1855, Frederick Douglass published his autobiography *My Bondage–My Freedom*.

In 1856, Wesleyan Methodist minister William Arthur printed a soul–stirring book of sermons, having an impact similar to Charles Finney's 1835 book *Lectures on Revivals of Religion.* William Arthur's book, titled *The Tongue of Fire, or true Power of Christianity,* was endorsed by the famous preacher Charles Spurgeon. It ended with a plea that God:

> ... crown this nineteenth century with a revival of pure and undefiled religion ...
> greater than any demonstration of the Spirit ever vouchsafed to man.

The next year, 1857, a financial panic occurred in America, the third major panic since the nation's founding. Banks failed, railroads went bankrupt, factories closed, and over 900 mercantile firms in New York went out of business. Even a farmer in St. Louis, former army captain Ulysses S. Grant, had to pawn his gold watch. Over 30,000 were out of work in New York City.

At this time, a businessman in New York, Jeremiah Lamphier, took a position as a lay missionary with the Dutch Reformed North Church near Fulton and William Streets.

He had been converted in 1842 at Charles Finney's Broadway Tabernacle in New York City. Lamphier began inviting merchants, clerks, mechanics and others to join him for noonday prayer for one hour on Wednesdays.

The first Wednesday, September 23, 1857, six people showed up. The next week 40. They decided to pray daily, and within six months, there were ten thousand participating in the Layman's Prayer Revival.

Spreading across the nation, there were over a million converts praying day and night in the next two years. Vice and crime decreased, criminals returned stolen money, wealthy helped the poor, sailors openly prayed, and when ungodly shipmates mocked them, the presence of God caused them to kneel in repentance. A religious journal reported March 1858:

> The large cities and towns from Maine to California are sharing in this great and glorious work. There is hardly a village or town to be found where "a special divine power" does not appear displayed.

Run by lay leadership, the revival spread:

• New York City – 50,000 of the city's 800,000 population became new converts;

• Utica, New York – daily prayer meetings filled the First Presbyterian Church, overflowing the balconies;

• Albany, New York – the New York State Capitol had prayer in the halls every morning beginning at 8:30am;

• Newark, New Jersey – 3,000 came to Christ, with nearby towns seeing almost their entire populations converted;

• Boston, Massachusetts – leading businessmen and commoners attended, as a witness recorded, "'Publicans and sinners' are awakened, and are entering the prayer meetings of their own accord. Some of them manifest signs of sincere repentance";

• Haverhill, Massachusetts – crowds came to the daily, weeping in repentance. Every family had someone seeking God;

• Washington, DC – prayer meetings held 5 times a day for scores of seekers;

• Philadelphia, Pennsylvania – 4,000 met in Jayne's Hall, as witnessed by philanthropist John Price Crozer, "I have never, I think, been present at a more stirring and edifying prayer meeting, the room quite full, and a divine influence seemed manifest. Many hearts melted, many souls devoutly engaged";

• Pittsburgh, Pennsylvania – 6,000 attended prayer meetings;

• Kalamazoo, Michigan – a woman wrote a prayer request to be read publicly at the meeting for her husband's salvation. When it was read, a man shouted, "Pray for me. I'm that man";

• Charleston, South Carolina – 2,000 prayed at Anson Street Presbyterian Church for over 8 weeks. One night, Dr. John Giradeaux dismissed the meeting, but no one left until midnight.

• Waco, Texas – as reported in The New York Observer, "Day and night the church has been crowded during the meeting ... Never before in Texas have we seen a whole community so effectually under a religious influence ... thoroughly regenerated";

• Louisville, Kentucky – 1,000 attended the daily union prayer, as one witness wrote, "The Spirit of God seems to be brooding over our city, and to have produced an unusual degree of tenderness and solemnity in all classes";

• Chicago, Illinois – 2,000 met for noon prayer in Metropolitan Hall, with a common business sign reading, "Will reopen at the close of the prayer meeting."

Professor J. Edwin Orr of Fuller Theological Seminary estimated that the 1858–59 Layman's Prayer Revival resulted in a sustained increase in church attendance, significant moral reform in society, and over a million Americans converting to faith in Christ.

Sometimes referred to as the beginning of a Third Great Awakening, the prayer revival gave birth to the Protestant social gospel movement to "civilize and Christianize" the world through charitable activities.

CR

SHOE SALESMAN TO EVANGELIST: DWIGHT L. MOODY
"FAITH MAKES ALL THINGS POSSIBLE,
LOVE MAKES ALL THINGS EASY"

During the Layman's Prayer Revival 1858, a traveling shoe salesman arrived in Chicago named Dwight Lyman Moody, working for the Wiswall Brothers.

His father had died when he was four, so he began working early, never finishing his education. Though raised a unitarian, he was converted to evangelical Christianity in 1855 by a Sunday school teacher. In Chicago, D.L. Moody began a Sunday School mission for underprivileged and immigrant children in the inner city, teaching in an abandoned saloon. William Reynolds wrote of visiting Moody's class:

> The first meeting I ever saw him at was in a little old shanty that had been abandoned by a saloon–keeper. Mr. Moody had got the place to hold the meetings in at night.

> I went there a little late; and the first thing I saw was a man standing up with a few tallow candles around him, holding a negro boy, and trying to read to him the story of the Prodigal Son and a great many words he could not read out, and had to skip. I thought, "If the Lord can ever use such an instrument as that for His honor and glory, it will astonish me."

After that meeting was over, Mr. Moody said to me, "Reynolds, I have got only one talent: I have no education, but I love the Lord Jesus Christ, and I want to do something for him, and I want you to pray for me."

Moody stated:

It is a masterpiece of the devil to make us believe that children cannot understand religion. Would Christ have made a child the standard of faith if He had known that it was not capable of understanding His words?

By 1860, D.L. Moody's Chicago Bible class had grown to over 1,000 attendees, with even President–elect Abraham Lincoln visiting on his way to Washington, DC., November 25, 1860. At Moody's prompting, Lincoln addressed the students:

I was once as poor as any boy in this school, but I am now President of the United States, and if you attend to what is taught you here, some of you may yet be President of the United States.

When the Civil War began in 1861, D.L. Moody joined the United States Christian Commission of the Y.M.C.A. to minister to the soldiers on the battlefields. Nine different times he was at the battlefront, including the Battle of Shiloh, Battle of Stones River, and was with General Grant's troops when they entered Richmond, Virginia.

After the war, he served as president of the Y.M.C.A. from 1865–1870. At the time, Chicago was the second biggest city in America, after New York City. D.L. Moody built the Illinois Street Church in Chicago, but it was destroyed in The Great Chicago Fire of 1871. The Great Chicago Fire destroyed an area four miles wide and a mile across.

With tornadoes of fire, it killed over 300 people, destroyed 17,000 buildings, and left 100,000 homeless. Tons of soot, ash and embers were carried by hurricane force winds across Lake Michigan, setting fires all across Michigan.

D.L. Moody said: "We can stand affliction better than we can prosperity, for in prosperity we forget God." He raised money and rebuilt the Y.M.C.A., and the Chicago Avenue Church. Attendance grew to over 10,000, with 6,000 waiting outside.

Moody preached to hundreds of thousands across America, holding evangelistic meetings from Boston to New York, to San Francisco and Vancouver. Even President U.S. Grant and his cabinet attended one of his meetings on January 19, 1876.

Moody began preaching to crowds in New York. Needing a large building, P.T. Barnum let Moody use his Great Roman Hippodrome, as his circus was not open on Sundays. When P.T. Barnum's show began traveling, D.L. Moody, with help from banker J.P. Morgan and railroad industrialist Cornelius Vanderbilt, transformed the Great Roman Hippodrome into a revival tabernacle.

Services began February 7, 1876, with 7,000 people in the main hall, 4,000 in overflow, thousands outside, 500 ushers and 1,200 singers directed by Ira Sankey. Sunday attendance hit 25,000. It was perhaps Moody's most important campaign, for in impacting New York, he impacted the world. Moody recorded an account:

> I remember when preaching in New York City, at the Hippodrome, a man coming up to me and telling me a story that thrilled my soul. One night, he said he had been gambling; had gambled all the money he had away. When he went home to the hotel

that night he did not sleep much.

The next morning happened to be Sunday. He got up, felt bad, couldn't eat anything, didn't touch his breakfast, was miserable, and thought about putting an end to his existence. That afternoon he took a walk up Broadway, and when he came to the Hippodrome he saw great crowds going in and thought of entering too ...

When inside he listened to the singing and heard the text, "Where art thou?" and he thought he would go out. He rose to go, and the text came upon his ears again, "Where art thou?" This was too personal, he thought, it was disagreeable, and he made for the door, but as he got to the third row from the entrance, the words came to him again. "Where art thou?" He stood still, for the question had come to him with irresistible force, and God had found him right there.

He went to his hotel and prayed all that night, and now he is a bright and shining light. And this young man, who was a commercial traveler, went back to the village in which he had been reared ... and went around among his friends and acquaintances and testified for Christ, as earnestly and beneficially for him as his conduct had (before) been against Him.

In 1892, Moody preached to tens of thousands in England at Charles Spurgeon's London Metropolitan Tabernacle. He also met with missionary to China, Hudson Taylor.

Afterwards, he and his son, Will, boarded the ocean liner *Spree* and headed for New York. Weak in health, he considered canceling his preaching at the 1893 Chicago World's Fair. On the third day of the voyage, there was a loud crash. A shock reverberated through the ship. The shaft had broken and the ship began to sink. Drifting for several days out of the sea lanes, all hope of being spotted by passing vessels faded. The ship was taking on so much water the pumps were useless. Lifeboats would capsize in the rough seas.

Passengers gathered on the slanted floor of the main saloon and waited for two days. Moody preached a message of faith to the crowd, and shortly afterwards, a ship was spotted coming to their rescue. After landing, he met with Bible students, saying:

> If you have any regard for me, if you love me, pray for me that God may anoint me for the work in Chicago; I want to be filled with the Spirit that I may preach the Gospel as I never preached it before; we want to see the salvation of God as we have never seen it before.

He later wrote:

> As I was preparing to leave London after my last visit there, I called upon a famous physician. He told me that my heart was weakening and that I would have to ease up on my work, that I would have to be more careful of myself; and I was going home with an idea that I would ease up a little.

> During the voyage, the announcement came that our vessel, the *Spree*, was sinking, and we rolled there for two days helplessly. No one on earth knows what I passed through at the thought that probably my work was finished, and that I would never again have the privilege of preaching the Gospel of Jesus Christ; and on that first dark night after the accident, I made a vow that if God would let me live and bring

me back to America, I would go back to Chicago, and at this World's Fair, preach the Gospel with all the power He would give me.

And God has made it possible for me to keep that vow during the past five months. It seems as if I went to the very gates of Heaven during that two days on the sinking ship, and God permitted me to come back and preach His Son a little longer.

D.L. Moody supported the Israeli settlement of their homeland. Moody's preaching at the Chicago World's Fair was the capstone of his ministry, as he wrote:

This has been by far the best week we have had. The Gospel has through this agency been brought to 150,000 people during the week. I have never seen greater eagerness to hear the word of God. The largest halls are too small for the crowds that come to many of the services.

One night ... (there) was a wonderful display of fireworks and illuminations, tens of thousands of people gazing on the scene. It seemed useless to expect any one to come away from that scene and sit down in a tabernacle to hear the Gospel; but the house was filled, and we had a blessed meeting. The following nights though cold and rainy ... people crowded in until every inch of space was occupied.

I thank God that I am living in Chicago today; these have been the happiest moments of my life; what a work He has given us today; what encouragements He has given us; how He has blessed us. Perhaps never in your life will some of you have an opportunity to do as much for Christ as now.

Moody preached to an estimated 100 million during his lifetime. He stated:

- There are many of us that are willing to do great things for the Lord, but few of us are willing to do little things.

- God doesn't seek for golden vessels ... but He must have clean ones.

- The Bible will keep you from sin, or sin will keep you from the Bible.

- I know the Bible is inspired because it inspires me.

- Faith makes all things possible ... Love makes all things easy.

- Death may be the King of terrors ... but Jesus is the King of kings!

- Preparation for old age should begin not later than one's teens. A life which is empty of purpose until 65 will not suddenly become filled on retirement.

- Treat the Lord Jesus Christ as a personal friend. His is not a creed, a mere doctrine, but it is He Himself we have.

D.L. Moody started the Chicago Bible Institute, renamed the Moody Bible Institute after his death, with R.A. Torrey as its president. The Chicago Avenue Church was renamed Moody Church in 1906 and continues its international impact with notable leaders such as pastor emeritus Dr. Erwin W. Lutzer. D.L. Moody stated:

> Moses spent 40 years thinking he was somebody; 40 years learning he was nobody; and 40 years discovering what God can do with a nobody.

FROM SLAVE TO COLLEGE PRESIDENT
"FEW THINGS CAN HELP AN INDIVIDUAL MORE THAN TO PLACE RESPONSIBILITY ON THEM"

Booker T. Washington was born in a slave hut on a plantation in Franklin County, Virginia, April 5, 1856. He taught himself to read and write, stating:

> In all my efforts to learn to read, my mother shared fully my ambition and sympathized with me and aided me in every way she could.

He attended school after working all day. At age 16, after the Civil War had ended, Booker T. Washington walked nearly 500 miles to attend the Hampton Institute in Virginia, founded by Union General Samuel Chapman Armstrong. Washington stated:

> I have spoken of my admiration for General Armstrong, and yet he was but a type of that Christ–like body of men and women who went into the Negro schools at the close of the war by the hundreds to assist in lifting up my race. The history of the world fails to show a higher, purer, and more unselfish class of men and women than those who found their way into those Negro schools.

Graduating from the Hampton Institute in 1875, Booker T. Washington wrote in his book, *Up From Slavery,* 1901:

> Perhaps the most valuable thing that I got out of my second year at the Hampton Institute was an understanding of the use and value of the Bible. Miss Nathalie Lord, one of the teachers, from Portland, Maine, taught me how to use and love the Bible ... I learned to love to read the Bible, not only for the spiritual help which it gives, but on account of it as literature.
>
> The lessons taught me in this respect took such a hold upon me that at the present time, when I am at home, no matter how busy I am, I always make it a rule to read a chapter or a portion of a chapter in the morning, before beginning the work of the day. Whatever ability I may have as a public speaker I owe in a measure to Miss Lord.

Booker T. Washington wrote in *The Story of My Life and Work* (1901):

> Aside from Gen. Armstrong ... the persons who made the deepest impression upon me at Hampton were Miss Nathalie Lord and Miss Elizabeth Brewer, two teachers from New England. I am especially indebted to these two for being helped in my spiritual life and led to love and understand the Bible. Largely by reason of their teaching, I find that a day rarely, if ever, passes when I am at home, that I do not read the Bible.

Miss Natalie Lord wrote in an article for the Hampton Institution publication, *The Southern Workman* (May 1902):

Booker, as we always called him ... I was much interested in him from the first. His quiet, unassuming manner, his earnestness of purpose and faithfulness greatly impressed me. I saw in him one whom you could completely trust. He was diligent in his business ... and yet unselfish in his thought for others.

Later, Booker T. Washington attended Wayland Baptist Seminary in Washington, DC. He then moved to West Virginia and worked in a salt furnace and coal mine. In 1876, he taught school in Malden, West Virginia, where he also taught a Sunday School class at the African Zion Baptist Church. He returned to teach at the Hampton Institute.

In 1881, at the age of 25, Booker T. Washington founded the Tuskegee Institute in Alabama with 33 students. Students not only had to learn academics, but also trade skills. They grew their own crops and raised livestock.

Washington observed that since slaves had been forced to work so hard on plantations, once freed, some held the expectation that they did not have to work as hard, even though they benefited from it. He countered this by teaching:

• No race can prosper until it learns that there is as much dignity in tilling a field as in writing a poem.

• I want to see you own land.

• What is equally important, each one of the students works ... each day at some industry, in order to get skill and the love of work, so that when he goes out from the institution he is prepared to set the people with whom he goes to labor a proper example in the matter of industry.

• Few things can help an individual more than to place responsibility on him, and to let him know that you trust him.

Booker T. Washington hired Robert Robinson Taylor, the first African–American architect from MIT, who graduated near the top of his class. Students made the bricks and helped build over 100 campus building, constructing classrooms, barns, outbuildings, and in 1899, Tuskegee's impressive chapel.

In the Spring of 1896, Booker T. Washington invited George Washington Carver to teach at Tuskegee, as he had just received his Master's Degree from Iowa State Agricultural Institute. Booker T. Washington became friends with the leading men of his day, including:

• Steel industrialist Andrew Carnegie;

• Standard Oil's John D. Rockefeller and Henry Huttleston Rogers;

• George Eastman, inventor and founder of Kodak; and

• Sears, Roebuck & Company President Julius Rosenwald.

Julius Rosenwald funded a pilot program of over 100 elementary schools, designed and operated by Tuskegee. Rosenwald and Carnegie took a "matching fund" approach to expand to 4,977 schools, 217 teacher homes and 163 shop buildings in 15 States. An Agricultural College on Wheels taught over 2,000 farmers in 28 States.

Booker T. Washington was thankful for rich people who supported his work at Tuskegee

(*Up From Slavery,* 1901):

> The more I come into contact with wealthy people, the more I believe that they are growing in the direction of looking upon their money simply as an instrument which God has placed in their hand for doing good with. I never go to the office of Mr. John D. Rockefeller, who more than once has been generous to Tuskegee, without being reminded of this. The close, careful, and minute investigation that he always makes in order to be sure that every dollar that he gives will do the most good — an investigation that is just as searching as if he were investing money in a business enterprise — convinces me that the growth in this direction is most encouraging.

Washington added:

> In the city of Boston I have rarely called upon an individual for funds that I have not been thanked for calling, usually before I could get an opportunity to thank the donor for the money ... The donors seem to feel, in a large degree, that an honor is being conferred upon them in their being permitted to give ... Nowhere else have I met with, in so large a measure, this fine and Christ–like spirit as in the city of Boston, although there are many notable instances of it outside that city. I repeat my belief that the world is growing in the direction of giving.

Booker T. Washington was grateful for the generosity of Christian churches, as he wrote in *Up From Slavery,* 1901:

> In my efforts to get money (for Tuskegee Institute) I have often been surprised at the patience and deep interest of the ministers, who are besieged on every hand

and at all hours of the day for help.

If no other consideration had convinced me of the value of the Christian life, the Christ–like work which the Church of all denominations in America has done during the last thirty-five years for the elevation of the black man would have made me a Christian.

In a large degree it has been the pennies, the nickels, and the dimes which have come from the Sunday–schools, the Christian Endeavor societies, and the missionary societies, as well as from the church proper, that have helped to elevate the Negro at so rapid a rate.

Booker T. Washington gave an address titled "The Place of the Bible in the Uplifting of the Negro Race," at Memorial Hall in Columbus, Ohio, May 24, 1900, as described in *The Booker T. Washington Papers,* Vol. 5: 1899–1900 (University of Illinois Press, ed. Louis R. Harlan and Raymond W. Smock, 1976, p. 543–544):

Dr. Washington walked on the stage at Memorial Hall with a firm, confident tread, as one sure of his ground. His shoulders are broad and six feet of stature gives strength and poise to command respect. His hair is close cut and gives him the aspect of a war dog with all its tenacious fighting spirit.

The eyes, however, gleam with kindliness and they temper the appearance of the latent fighting forces ... His jaw has the firmness of one who has the courage to stand by his convictions ...

The description continued:

"It's easy to see how that man succeeds," whispered a delegate to the Bible students' conference after looking at the speaker.

John R. Mott, general secretary of the student movement of North America, presided at the afternoon meeting at Memorial Hall ... Mr. Mott announced Dr. Washington's subject as "The Place of the Bible in the Uplifting of the Negro Race." Dr. Washington began his address after a quartet sang.

He spoke of the 91 Y.M.C.A. Organizations for colored youths; of the 5000 colored men studying the Bible, and of the 640 Bible students at Tuskegee, and pointed these as living examples of the progress of the Negro. He pleaded for two more secretaries to teach Bible in the South–land.

Booker T. Washington spoke from New Hampshire to California, Minnesota to Florida. In 1899, he and his wife traveled to Europe, where they met many dignitaries, including being honored by an invitation to Windsor Castle in England for tea with Queen Victoria.

Booker T. Washington wrote in his autobiography *Up From Slavery* (1901):

Through the kindness of Lady Aberdeen, my wife and I were enabled ... to see Queen Victoria, at Windsor Castle, where, afterward, we were all the guests of her Majesty at tea. In our party was Miss Susan B. Anthony, and I was deeply impressed with the fact that one did not often get an opportunity to see, during the same hour, two women so remarkable in different ways as Susan B. Anthony and Queen Victoria.

Washington believed that to be great, one should read the Bible, (*The Booker T. Washington Papers*, Vol. 3: 1889–95, ed., Louis R. Harlan, University of Illinois Press, 1974, p. 93):

> As a rule a person should get into the habit of reading his Bible. You never read in history of any great man whose influence has been lasting, who has not been a reader of the Bible. Take Abraham Lincoln and Gladstone (British Prime Minister). Their lives show that they have been readers of the Bible. If you wish to properly direct your mind and necessarily your lives, begin by reading the book of all books.

> Read your Bible every day, and you will find how healthily you will grow.

In his address at Columbus, Ohio, May 24, 1900, Booker T. Washington stated:

> The men doing the vital things of life are those who read the Bible and are Christians and not ashamed to let the world know it.

He added:

> Those who have accomplished the greatest results are those ... who never grow excited or lose self–control, but are always calm, self-possessed, patient and polite.

Booker T. Washington believed a religious life was key to freedom, usefulness and honor, as he wrote in *Putting the Most into Life* (NY: Thomas Y. Crowell & Co., 1906, chapter "Making Religion a Vital Part of Living," p. 23–25):

> Educated men and women, especially those who are in college, very often get the idea that religion is fit only for the common people. No young man or woman can make a greater error than this ...

My observation has taught me that the people who stand for the most in the educational and commercial world and in the uplifting of the people are in some real way connected with the religious life of the people among whom they reside. This being true we ought to make the most of our religious life ...

He continued:

First the habit of regular attendance at some religious service should be cultivated. This is one of the outward helps toward inward grace ... As you value your spiritual life, see to it that you do not lose the spirit of reverence for the Most High ...

Do not mistake denominationalism for reverence and religion. Religion is life, denominationalism is an aid to life ... Systematic reading and prayerful study of the Bible is the second outward help which I would commend to those whom I wish to see make the most of their spiritual life.

Many people regard the Bible as a wonderful piece of literature only ...

Nowhere in all literature can be found a finer bit of oratory than St. Paul's defense before King Agrippa. But praiseworthy as this kind of study is, I do not believe it is sufficient. The Bible should be read as a daily guide to right living and as a daily incentive to positive Christian service ...

Washington went on:

To live the real religious life is in some measure to share the character of God. The word "atonement," which occurs in the Bible again and again, means literally at–one–ment. To be at one with God is to be like God.

Our real religious striving, then, should be to become one with God, sharing with Him in our poor human way His qualities and attributes. To do this, we must get the inner life, the heart right, and we shall then become stronger where we have been weak, wise where we have been foolish ...

Washington concluded:

We must learn to incorporate God's laws into our thoughts and words and acts. Frequent reference is made in the Bible to the freedom that comes from being a Christian. A man is free just in proportion as he learns to live within God's laws ... As we learn God's laws and grow into His likeness we shall find our reward in this world in a life of usefulness and honor. To do this is to have found the kingdom of God, which is the kingdom of character and righteousness and peace.

Booker T. Washington stated in "The Place of the Bible in the Uplifting of the Negro Race," Memorial Hall in Columbus, Ohio, May 24, 1900:

The Negro who does the shooting is uneducated and without Christian training ... Of all the graduates from Tuskegee Institute only one had been since sentenced to the penitentiary ... So the work today is to make religion the vital part of the Negro's life. But this is a stupendous task, as there is a nation of Negros ...

He added:

Just remember that the Negro came out of Africa a few centuries ago ... with chains upon his ankles and wrists. He came out of that, clothed according to civilized customs with a hammer and a saw ... and a Bible in his hands. No man can read the Bible and be lazy. Christianity increases a man's ... capacity for labor. The Negro doesn't run from the Bible, either.

Washington continued describing Tuskegee Institute:

While the institution is in no sense denominational, we have a department known as the Phelps Hall Bible Training School, in which a number of students are prepared for the ministry and other forms of Christian work, especially work in the country districts ...

In the school we made a special effort to teach our students the meaning of Christmas, and to give them lessons in its proper observance ... The Season now has a new meaning, not only through all that immediate region, but ... wherever our graduates have gone.

Washington wrote in *Up From Slavery,* 1901:

When speaking directly in the interests of the Tuskegee Institute, I usually arrange, sometime in advance, a series of meetings in important centers. This takes me before churches, Sunday–schools, Christian Endeavour Societies, and men's and women's clubs. When doing this I sometimes speak before as many as four organizations in a single day ...

He continued:

While a great deal of stress is laid upon the industrial side of the work at Tuskegee, we do not neglect or overlook in any degree, the religious and spiritual side. The school is strictly undenominational, but it is thoroughly Christian, and the spiritual training of the students is not neglected.

Our preaching service, prayer–meetings, Sunday–school, Christian Endeavor Society, Young Men's Christian Association, and various missionary organizations, testify to this ...

He added:

You may fill your heads with knowledge or skillfully train your hands, but unless it is based upon high upright character, upon a true heart, it will amount to nothing. Though Tuskegee was non-sectarian, its daily life was permeated by active religion which included Sunday preaching services and Sunday school classes, daily evening chapel devotionals and a "Week of Prayer" held for two weeks every January.

A Bible Training school was established in 1893 to prepare students for Christian ministry. Students helped out at community churches on Sundays; ran a Y.M.C.A. that looked after the sick, needy, and elderly in the area; and staffed a Humane Society for the proper care of animals.

CR

BOOKER T. WASHINGTON'S WISDOM & WORLD INFLUENCE "BY 1905, TUSKEGEE PRODUCED MORE SELF–MADE MILLIONAIRES THAN HARVARD, YALE, & PRINCETON"

In 1905, visitors came to Tuskegee from 16 countries, including Africa, India, China, Japan, Poland and Russia. Booker T. Washington sent Tuskegee graduates to Liberia, West Africa. He even sent his personal envoy, Emmett Scott, to discourage France from annexing Liberia, helping to preserve Liberia's independence.

During Booker T. Washington's lifetime, Tuskegee Institute grew to 2,000 students and a faculty of 200 teaching 38 trades. He met with and advised Presidents William McKinley, Theodore Roosevelt, William H. Taft, and Calvin Coolidge.

Booker T. Washington was the first African American to have his image on a U.S. postage stamp, 1940. In 1945, he was the first African American elected to the Hall of Fame, and in 1946, his image was placed on a U.S. Coin.

In 1896, Booker T. Washington was awarded an honorary master's degree from Harvard, the first New England university to confer an honorary degree upon a black man. Harvard President Charles W. Eliot wrote May 28, 1896:

President Booker T. Washington,

My Dear Sir, Harvard University desires to confer on you at the approaching Commencement an honorary degree; but it is our custom to confer degrees only on gentlemen who are present. Our Commencement occurs this year on June 24, and your presence would be desirable from about noon until about five o'clock in the afternoon. Would it be possible for you to be in Cambridge on that day? Believe me, with great regard, Very truly yours, Charles W. Eliot.

Harvard President Charles W. Eliot spoke at Tuskegee's 25th anniversary in 1906, stating: "By 1905, Tuskegee produced more self–made millionaires than Harvard, Yale and Princeton combined."

Booker T. Washington was awarded an honorary doctorate from Dartmouth in 1901. Many places and items were named for him, including: a bridge, a mountain, a ship, an airplane, a stamp, a coin, a college, parks, buildings, elementary schools, middle schools, and high schools.

In November of 1897, Booker T. Washington arrived at the White House and met President William McKinley. He wrote:

In a few minutes word came from Mr. McKinley that he would see me. How any man can see so many people ... and still keep himself calm, patient, and fresh for each visitor in the way that President McKinley does, I cannot understand. When I saw the President he kindly thanked me for the work which we were doing at Tuskegee for the interests of the country.

I then told him, briefly, the object of my visit. I impressed upon him the fact that a visit from the Chief Executive of the Nation would not only encourage our students and teachers, but would help the entire race.

Washington wrote further:

I went to Washington again and saw him, with a view of getting him to extend his trip to Tuskegee. On this second visit Mr. Charles W. Hare, a prominent white citizen of Tuskegee, kindly volunteered to accompany me, to reinforce my invitation with one from the white people of Tuskegee and the vicinity ... I saw the President ... I perceived that his heart was greatly burdened by reason of these race disturbances.

Although there were many people waiting to see him, he detained me for some time, discussing the condition and prospects of the race. He remarked several times that he was determined to show his interest and faith in the race, not merely in words, but by acts.

Washington continued:

The President promised that he would visit our school on the 16th of December ... When it became known that the President was going to visit our school, the white citizens of the town of Tuskegee — a mile distant from the school — were as much pleased as were our students and teachers.

The white people of the town, including both men and women, began arranging to decorate the town ... I think I never realized before this how much the white people of Tuskegee and vicinity thought of our institution ... Dozens of these people came to me and said ... if there was anything they could do to help, or to relieve me personally, I had but to intimate [suggest] it and they would be only too glad to assist ...

The thing that touched me almost as deeply as the visit of the President itself was the deep pride which all classes of citizens in Alabama seemed to take in our work.

Washington continued:

The morning of December 16th brought to the little city of Tuskegee such a crowd as it had never seen before. With the President came Mrs. McKinley and all of the Cabinet officers but one; and most of them brought their wives or some members of their families ...

There was also a host of newspaper correspondents. The Alabama Legislature was in session at Montgomery at this time. This body passed a resolution to adjourn for the purpose of visiting Tuskegee ...

The citizens of Tuskegee had decorated the town from the station to the school in a generous manner. In order to economize in the matter of time, we arranged to have the whole school pass in review before the President.

Each student carried a stalk of sugar–cane with some open bolls of cotton fastened to the end of it. Following the students, the work of all departments of the school passed in review, displayed on "floats" drawn by horses, mules, and oxen ...

In his address in our large, new chapel, which the students had recently completed, the President (McKinley) said:

"Tuskegee Normal and Industrial Institute is ideal in its conception, and has already a large and growing reputation in the country, and is not unknown abroad. I congratulate all who are associated in this undertaking for the good work which it is doing in the education of its students to lead lives of honor and usefulness, thus exalting the race for which it was established ...

To speak of Tuskegee without paying special tribute to Booker T. Washington's genius and perseverance would be impossible. The inception of this noble enterprise was his, and he deserves high credit for it. His was the enthusiasm and enterprise which made its steady progress possible and established in the institution its present high standard of accomplishment. He has won a worthy reputation as one of the great leaders of his race, widely known and much respected at home and abroad as an accomplished educator, a great orator, and a true philanthropist."

Secretary of the Navy John D. Long then spoke in honor of Booker T. Washington at Tuskegee:

I cannot make a speech today. My heart is too full—full of hope, admiration, and pride for my countrymen of both sections and both colors. I am filled with gratitude and admiration for your work, and from this time forward I shall have absolute confidence in your progress and in the solution of the problem in which you are engaged. The problem, I say, has been solved ...

A picture has been presented today which should be put upon canvas with the pictures of Washington and Lincoln, and transmitted to future time and generations – a picture which the press of the country should spread broadcast over the land, a most dramatic picture, and that picture is this:

"The President of the United States standing on this platform; on one side the Governor of Alabama, on the other, completing the trinity, a representative of a race only a few years ago in bondage, the colored President of the Tuskegee Normal and Industrial Institute."

Navy Secretary Long concluded:

God bless the President under whose majesty such a scene as that is presented to the American people. God bless the state of Alabama, which is showing that it can deal with this problem for itself. God bless the orator, philanthropist, and disciple of the Great Master — who, if he were on earth, would be doing the same work — Booker T. Washington.

John D. Long wrote to his wife, Agnes Pierce Long, during the Spanish–American War, October 9, 1898:

The Tenth Regular Infantry ... is composed, with the exception of the officers, entirely of colored men. It is one of the regiments which did the very best work in the Santiago campaign, and no soldiers fought better ...

They marched with an easy light step; they had the faces of their race. It was a great day for them and for the colored people who cheered them on the way ... I could not help thinking of this race a few years ago in slavery and today freemen and citizens.

How barbarous seems the color discrimination, when in every walk of life they are making the same progress as the white man; when their Booker T. Washington is, perhaps, the finest orator in the country and these troops the best fighting soldiers of the war.

After the Civil War, freed slaves began to advance in society, but Democrat vigilante groups in the South tried to keep them down, committing over 4,000 lynchings. The Tuskegee Institute recorded that from 1882–1968, 3,446 blacks and 1,297 whites were lynched –the whites being "radical" Republicans who were caught registering freed blacks to vote.

To the protests of some Democrats, Republican President Theodore Roosevelt had Booker T. Washington as an honored guest for dinner at the White House, October 16, 1901. The Southern Democrat newspaper *The Memphis Scimitar* printed:

The most damnable outrage which has ever been perpetrated by any citizen of the United States was committed yesterday by the President, when he invited a n——— to dine with him at the White House. It would not be worth more than a passing notice if Theodore Roosevelt had sat down to dinner in his own home with a Pullman car porter, but Roosevelt the individual and Roosevelt the President are not to be viewed in the same light.

Booker T. Washington wrote in *Up From Slavery* (1901):

I learned this lesson from General Samuel Chapman Armstrong, and resolved that I would permit no man, no matter what his color might be, to narrow and degrade my soul by making me hate him. With God's help, I believe that I have completely rid myself of any ill feeling toward the Southern white man for any wrong that he may have inflicted upon my race.

I am made to feel just as happy now when I am rendering service to Southern white men as when the service is rendered to a member of my own race. I pity from the bottom of my heart any individual who is so unfortunate as to get into the habit of holding race prejudice.

Washington stated:

• In the sight of God there is no color line, and we want to cultivate a spirit that will make us forget that there is such a line anyway.

• I have always had the greatest respect for the work of the Salvation Army especially because I have noted that it draws no color line in religion.

Booker T. Washington wrote:

The man is unwise who does not cultivate in every manly way the friendship and goodwill of his next–door neighbor, whether he be black or white.

Tuskegee Professor George Washington Carver wrote to Robert Johnson, March 24, 1925: "Thank God I love humanity; complexion doesn't interest me one single bit."

George W. Carver wrote to YMCA official Jack Boyd in Denver, March 1, 1927:

> Keep your hand in that of the Master, walk daily by His side, so that you may lead others into the realms of true happiness, where a religion of hate, (which poisons both body and soul) will be unknown, having in its place the "Golden Rule" way, which is the "Jesus Way" of life, will reign supreme.

Booker T. Washington wrote in *Up From Slavery* (1901):

> Great men cultivate love ... Only little men cherish a spirit of hatred.

He had to walk a fine line between: racist Southern Democrats who committed violence if blacks tried to advance their social and economic status; and the Northern black activists who were insensitive to his precarious situation in the Democrat South and criticized him for not demanding Democrat reparations.

Such was W.E.B. Dubois, who later visited Mao Zedung and joined the Communist Party. Booker T. Washington warned in *My Larger Education–Being Chapters from My Experience* (1911, chapter V: The Intellectuals and the Boston Mob, p. 118):

> There is another class of colored people who make a business of keeping the troubles, the wrongs, and the hardships of the Negro race before the public. Having learned that they are able to make a living out of their troubles, they have grown into the settled habit of advertising their wrongs – partly because they want sympathy and partly because it pays. Some of these people do not want the Negro to lose his grievances, because they do not want to lose their jobs ...

There is a certain class of race–problem solvers who do not want the patient to get well, because as long as the disease holds out they have not only an easy means of making a living, but also an easy medium through which to make themselves prominent before the public.

Booker T. Washington stated: "A whining crying race may be pitied but seldom respected." His approach for blacks being fully accepted into American life was to follow the path immigrants took. German, Irish, Jewish, Polish, Italian, and others immigrated into America at the bottom of the social ladder, being met with racial discrimination. But by hard work, pooling of their efforts, they became educated, started businesses, accumulated wealth, made contributions to society, and rose in public respect. Washington stated:

> At the bottom of education, at the bottom of politics, even at the bottom of religion itself, there must be for our race, as for all races, an economic foundation, economic prosperity, economic independence.

> Leaders have devoted themselves to politics, little knowing, it seems, that political independence disappears without economic independence; that economic independence is the foundation of political independence.

Booker T. Washington recommended efforts to "concentrate all their energies on industrial education, and accumulation of wealth, and the conciliation of the South," believing that "Blacks would eventually gain full participation in society by showing themselves to be responsible, reliable American citizens." He wrote:

• No man who continues to add something to the material, intellectual and moral well-being of the place in which he lives is left without proper reward.

• I want to see my race live such high and useful lives that they will not be merely tolerated, but they shall be needed and wanted.

Ten years before the U.S. Chamber of Commerce was formed, Booker T. Washington founded the National Negro Business League in 1900, growing it to 600 chapters. He stated:

Anyone can seek a job, but it requires a person of rare ability to create a job ... What we should do in our schools is to turn out fewer job seekers and more job creators.

Widowed twice, his third wife outlived him. He had one daughter, Portia, and two sons, Booker T. Washington Jr. and Ernest Davidson Washington. When Booker T. Washington died on November 14, 1915, industrialist Andrew Carnegie stated:

I mourn with you today as one who shares your sorrow. America has lost one of her best and greatest citizens. History is to tell of two Washingtons. One the leader of his country and the other the leader of his race.

After Washington's death, Republican Vice-President Calvin Coolidge traveled to Tuskegee in 1923. He met with Robert Russa Moton, who succeeded Booker T. Washington as the principal of Tuskegee Institute. After becoming President of the United States, Calvin Coolidge received Robert Russa Moton at a meeting in the White House in 1924. Robert Russa Moton went on to be an advisor to five U.S. Presidents.

One of Booker T. Washington's most famous addresses was September 18, 1895, at the International Exposition in Atlanta. He explained:

> Atlanta was literally packed, at the time, with people from all parts of the country, and with representatives of foreign governments, as well as with military and civic organizations. The afternoon papers had forecasts of the next day's proceedings in flaring headlines. All this tended to add to my burden. I did not sleep much that night.

> The next morning, before day, I went carefully over what I planned to say. I also kneeled down and asked God's blessing upon my effort. Right here, perhaps, I ought to add that I make it a rule never to go before an audience, on any occasion, without asking the blessing of God upon what I want to say ...

Washington continued:

> A ship lost at sea for many days suddenly sighted a friendly vessel. From the mast of the unfortunate vessel was seen a signal, "Water, water; we die of thirst!" The answer from the friendly vessel at once came back, "Cast down your bucket where you are."

> A second time the signal, "Water, water; send us water!" ran up from the distressed vessel, and was answered, "Cast down your bucket where you are." And a third and fourth signal for water was answered, "Cast down your bucket where you are."

> The captain of the distressed vessel, at last heading the injunction, cast down his bucket, and it came up full of fresh, sparkling water from the mouth of the Amazon River.

Of note, is that the Amazon River is the longest river in the world, stretching across 4,345 miles. It is nearly 110 miles wide where it enters into the Atlantic Ocean, discharging up to 11 million cubic feet of water per second. It is so powerful that it pushes a stream of fresh water, 100 miles wide, out into the ocean for 250 miles.

Booker T. Washington continued his Atlanta address:

> To those of my race who depend on bettering their condition in a foreign land or who underestimate the importance of cultivating friendly relations with the Southern white man, who is their next–door neighbor, I would say: "Cast down your bucket where you are" – cast it down in making friends in every manly way of the people of all races by whom we are surrounded ...

He continued:

> To those of the white race who look to the incoming of those of foreign birth and strange tongue and habits of the prosperity of the South, were I permitted I would repeat what I say to my own race: "Cast down your bucket where you are." Cast it down among the eight millions of Negroes whose habits you know, whose fidelity and love you have tested.

Urging racial reconciliation, Booker T. Washington stated: "Opportunities never come a second time, nor do they wait for our leisure." He stated: "If you want to lift yourself up, lift up someone else."

CR

KATHERINE LEE BATES & "AMERICA THE BEAUTIFUL" "GOD SHED HIS GRACE ON THEE"

Almost chosen as the National Anthem in 1926, "America the Beautiful" was written by Katherine Lee Bates, born August 12, 1859.

Daughter of a Congregational minister, Katherine Lee Bates taught high school, then English literature at Wellesley College. She hosted gatherings at her home for students and literary guests, including Robert Frost, Carl Sandburg and William Butler Yeats.

Of her 1893 Colorado journey, Katherine Lee Bates wrote:

> Some of the other teachers and I decided to go on a trip to 14,000–foot Pikes Peak. We hired a prairie wagon. Near the top we had to leave the wagon and go the rest of the way on mules. I was very tired.

> But when I saw the view, I felt great joy. All the wonder of America seemed displayed there, with the sea–like expanse.

"America, the Beautiful" was quoted by President Johnson in his first address before a joint session of Congress, Supreme Court Justices and the Cabinet, November 27, 1963:

> John Kennedy's death commands what his life conveyed–that America must move

forward. The time has come for Americans of all races and creeds and political beliefs to understand and to respect one another ...

Let us here highly resolve that John Fitzgerald Kennedy did not live–or die–in vain ... As we gather together to ask the Lord's blessings and give Him our thanks, let us unite in those familiar and cherished words: "America, America, God shed His grace on thee, And crown thy good, With brotherhood, From sea to shining sea."

President Reagan met South Korean President Chun Doo Hwan, November 14, 1983:

At the worship service Sunday morning with our soldiers ... less than a mile from one of the most tyrannical regimes on Earth ... a choir of little girls ... all orphans ... closing the service, singing "America, the Beautiful" in our language, was a spiritual experience.

Bates' poem was printed in *The Congregationalist* for Independence Day, July 4, 1895:

O Beautiful for Spacious Skies,
For Amber Waves of Grain,
For Purple Mountain Majesties
Above the Fruited Plain!

America! America!
God Shed His Grace on Thee
And Crown Thy Good with Brotherhood
From Sea to Shining Sea!

O Beautiful for Pilgrim Feet,
Whose Stern Impassioned Stress
A Thoroughfare for Freedom Beat
Across the Wilderness!

America! America!
God Mend Thy Every Flaw,
Confirm Thy Soul in Self–Control
Thy Liberty in Law!

O Beautiful for Heroes Proved
In Liberating Strife,
Who More Than Self Their Country Loved,
And Mercy More Than Life!
　America! America!
May God Thy Gold Refine
Till All Success Be Nobleness
And Every Gain Divine!

O Beautiful for Patriots Dream
That Sees Beyond the Years
Thine Alabaster Cities Gleam
Undimmed by Human Tears!
　America! America!
God Shed His Grace on Thee
And Crown Thy Good With Brotherhood
From Sea to Shining Sea!

God shed His grace from sea to shining sea, as all 50 states, at some time in their history, acknowledged God somewhere in their constitution:

ALABAMA 1901, Preamble. We the people of the State of Alabama ... invoking the favor and guidance of Almighty God, do ordain and establish the following Constitution;

ALASKA 1956, Preamble. We, the people of Alaska, grateful to God and to those who founded our nation and pioneered this great land;

ARIZONA 1911, Preamble. We, the people of the State of Arizona, grateful to Almighty God for our liberties, do ordain this Constitution;

ARKANSAS 1874, Preamble. We, the people of the State of Arkansas, grateful to Almighty God for the privilege of choosing our own form of government;

CALIFORNIA 1879, Preamble. We, the People of the State of California, grateful to Almighty God for our freedom;

COLORADO 1876, Preamble. We, the people of Colorado, with profound reverence for the Supreme Ruler of Universe;

CONNECTICUT 1818, Preamble. The People of Connecticut, acknowledging with gratitude the good Providence of God in permitting them to enjoy;

DELAWARE 1897, Preamble. Through Divine Goodness all men have, by nature, the rights of worshiping and serving their Creator according to the dictates of their consciences;

FLORIDA 1885, Preamble. We, the people of the State of Florida, grateful to Almighty God for our constitutional liberty ... establish this Constitution;

GEORGIA 1777, Preamble. We, the people of Georgia, relying upon protection and guidance of Almighty God, do ordain and establish this Constitution;

HAWAII 1959, Preamble. We, the people of Hawaii, Grateful for Divine Guidance ... establish this Constitution;

IDAHO 1889, Preamble. We, the people of the State of Idaho, grateful to Almighty God for our freedom, to secure its blessings and promote our common welfare do establish this Constitution;

ILLINOIS 1870, Preamble. We, the people of the State of Illinois, grateful to Almighty

God for the civil, political and religious liberty which He hath so long permitted us to enjoy and looking to Him for a blessing on our endeavors;

INDIANA 1851, Preamble. We, the People of the State of Indiana, grateful to Almighty God for the free exercise of the right to chose our form of government;

IOWA 1857, Preamble. We, the People of the State of Iowa, grateful to the Supreme Being for the blessings hitherto enjoyed, and feeling our dependence on Him for a continuation of these blessings ... establish this Constitution;

KANSAS 1859, Preamble. We, the people of Kansas, grateful to Almighty God for our civil and religious privileges ... establish this Constitution;

KENTUCKY 1891, Preamble. We, the people of the Commonwealth of Kentucky, grateful to Almighty God for the civil, political and religious liberties;

LOUISIANA 1921, Preamble. We, the people of the State of Louisiana, grateful to Almighty God for the civil, political and religious liberties we enjoy;

MAINE 1820, Preamble. We the People of Maine ... acknowledging with grateful hearts the goodness of the Sovereign Ruler of the Universe in affording us an opportunity ... and imploring His aid and direction;

MARYLAND 1776, Preamble. We, the people of the state of Maryland, grateful to Almighty God for our civil and religious liberty;

MASSACHUSETTS 1780, Preamble. We ... the people of Massachusetts, acknowledging with grateful hearts, the goodness of the Great Legislator of the Universe ... in the course of His Providence, an opportunity ... and devoutly imploring His direction;

MICHIGAN 1908, Preamble. We, the people of the State of Michigan, grateful to Almighty God for the blessings of freedom ... establish this Constitution;

MINNESOTA 1857, Preamble. We, the people of the State of Minnesota, grateful to God for our civil and religious liberty, and desiring to perpetuate its blessings;

MISSISSIPPI 1890, Preamble. We, the people of Mississippi in convention assembled, grateful to Almighty God, and invoking His blessing on our work;

MISSOURI 1945, Preamble. We, the people of Missouri, with profound reverence for the Supreme Ruler of the Universe, and grateful for His goodness ... establish this Constitution;

MONTANA 1889, Preamble. We, the people of Montana, grateful to Almighty God for the blessings of liberty ... establish this Constitution;

NEBRASKA 1875, Preamble. We, the people, grateful to Almighty God for our freedom ... establish this Constitution;

NEVADA 1864, Preamble. We the people of the State of Nevada, grateful to Almighty God for our freedom ... establish this Constitution;

NEW HAMPSHIRE 1792, Part I. Art. I. Sec. V. Every individual has a natural and unalienable right to worship God according to the dictates of his own conscience;

NEW JERSEY 1844, Preamble. We, the people of the State of New Jersey, grateful to Almighty God for civil and religious liberty which He hath so long permitted us to enjoy, and looking to Him for a blessing on our endeavors;

NEW MEXICO 1911, Preamble. We, the People of New Mexico, grateful to Almighty God for the blessings of liberty;

NEW YORK 1846, Preamble. We, the people of the State of New York, grateful to Almighty God for our freedom, in order to secure its blessings;

NORTH CAROLINA 1868, Preamble. We the people of the State of North Carolina, grateful to Almighty God, the Sovereign Ruler of Nations, for ... our civil, political, and religious liberties, and acknowledging our dependence upon Him for the continuance of those;

NORTH DAKOTA 1889, Preamble. We, the people of North Dakota, grateful to Almighty God for the blessings of civil and religious liberty, do ordain;

OHIO 1852, Preamble. We the people of the state of Ohio, grateful to Almighty God for our freedom, to secure its blessings and to promote our common;

OKLAHOMA 1907, Preamble. Invoking the guidance of Almighty God, in order to secure and perpetuate the blessings of liberty ... establish this;

OREGON 1857, Bill of Rights, Article I. Section 2. All men shall be secure in the natural right, to worship Almighty God according to the dictates of their consciences;

PENNSYLVANIA 1776, Preamble. We, the people of Pennsylvania, grateful to Almighty God for the blessings of civil and religious liberty, and humbly invoking His guidance;

RHODE ISLAND 1842, Preamble. We the People of the State of Rhode Island ... grateful to Almighty God for the civil and religious liberty which He hath so long permitted us to enjoy, and looking to Him for a blessing;

SOUTH CAROLINA 1778, Preamble. We, the people of the State of South Carolina ... grateful to God for our liberties, do ordain and establish this Constitution;

SOUTH DAKOTA 1889, Preamble. We, the people of South Dakota, grateful to Almighty God for our civil and religious liberties ... establish this Constitution;

TENNESSEE 1796, Art. XI.III. That all men have a natural and indefeasible right to worship Almighty God according to the dictates of their conscience;

TEXAS 1845, Preamble. We the People of the Republic of Texas, acknowledging, with gratitude, the grace and beneficence of God;

UTAH 1896, Preamble. Grateful to Almighty God for life and liberty, we ... establish this Constitution;

VERMONT 1777, Preamble. Whereas all government ought to ... enable the individuals who compose it to enjoy their natural rights, and other blessings which the Author of Existence has bestowed on man;

VIRGINIA 1776, Bill of Rights, XVI ... Religion, or the Duty which we owe our

Creator ... can be directed only by Reason ... and that it is the mutual duty of all to practice Christian Forbearance, Love and Charity towards each other;

WASHINGTON 1889, Preamble. We the People of the State of Washington, grateful to the Supreme Ruler of the Universe for our liberties, do ordain this Constitution;

WEST VIRGINIA 1872, Preamble. Since through Divine Providence we enjoy the blessings of civil, political and religious liberty, we, the people of West Virginia ... reaffirm our faith in and constant reliance upon God;

WISCONSIN 1848, Preamble. We, the people of Wisconsin, grateful to Almighty God for our freedom, domestic tranquility;

WYOMING 1890, Preamble. We, the people of the State of Wyoming, grateful to God for our civil, political, and religious liberties ... establish this Constitution.

After reviewing acknowledgments of God from all 50 state constitutions, one is faced with the prospect that maybe, just maybe, the ACLU and the out–of–control federal courts are wrong.

CR

BASEBALL STAR TO NATIONAL PREACHER: BILLY SUNDAY "STAND UP & LET PEOPLE KNOW YOU STAND FOR JESUS ... HE WILL USE EACH OF US FOR HIS GLORY IF WE ONLY LET HIM"

A baseball star, Billy Sunday played for the Chicago White Stockings in the 1880s and later the Philadelphia Phillies.

Born during the Civil War in a log cabin in Iowa, his father, who was a Union Army soldier, died of pneumonia when Billy was a month old. He wrote in his autobiography, "I never saw my father." During his childhood, there were ten deaths among his relatives. Poverty led his mother to send him and his siblings to the Soldier's Orphans Home.

At age 15, Billy Sunday struck out on his own, working several jobs before playing baseball. His career took off when he was recruited by A.G. Spalding, owner of the White Stockings and founder of Spalding Sporting Goods Company. Billy Sunday became one of the most popular athletes in the nation.

While leaving a Chicago saloon with some other players in 1886, he heard a group of gospel singers on the street from the Pacific Garden Mission. Attracted by the hymns, as they were the same ones his mother used to sing, Billy Sunday went closer to listen.

He attended services at the mission and experienced a conversion, becoming an evangelical Christian. Billy began attending YMCA meetings and quit drinking. That same year, he went to Jefferson Park Presbyterian Church where he was introduced to Helen Amelia "Nell" Thompson.

Her father disapproved, considering baseball players "transient ne'er–do–wells who were unstable and destined to be misfits once they were too old to play." Her father eventually relented, gave his blessing, and Billy and Nell were married September 5, 1888.

Nell encouraged Billy, who was naturally shy, to begin speaking. She went on to organize all of his evangelistic meetings, with him admitting to "never yet gone contrary to Mrs. Sunday's advice."

Billy Sunday gave up making $5,000 a year as a professional baseball player to working at the YMCA (Young Men's Christian Association) for $75 a month. On February 17, 1889, a national sensation occurred when Billy Sunday preached his first sermon as a Christian evangelist in Chicago. The local press reported in sports' terms:

> Center fielder Billy Sunday made a three–base hit at Farwell Hall last night. There is no other way to express the success of his first appearance as an evangelist in Chicago. His audience was made up of about 500 men who didn't know much about his talents as a preacher but could remember his galloping to second base with his cap in hand.

During the next 46 years, until his death November 6, 1935, over 100 million people heard Billy Sunday preach.

His preaching carried on the revival tradition of:
- Scotland revivals beginning in the 1730s;
- First Great Awakening preaching of George Whitefield;
- Second Great Awakening camp meetings;
- pre–Civil War preaching of Charles Finney;
- 1857 New York City's Noontime Businessmen Prayer Meeting Revival led by Jeremiah Lamphier;
- post–Civil War evangelist D.L. Moody; and
- Welsh revivals at the turn of the last century.

Sunday proclaimed in Des Moines, Iowa, November 3, 1914:

When may a revival be expected? When the wickedness of the wicked grieves and distresses the Christian ...

What a spell the devil seems to cast over the church today! ...

If the church was down on her face in prayer they would be more concerned with the fellow outside. The church has degenerated into a third–rate amusement joint ...

It is as much the duty of the church to awaken ... men and women of this city as it is the duty of the fire department to arouse when the call sounds.

What would you think of the fire department of Des Moines if it slept while the town burned? You would condemn them and I will condemn you if you sleep and let men and women go to hell ...

Sunday added:

Christians have lost the spirit of prayer ... Religion needs a baptism of horse sense ... If you go to a farmer and say ... God will give you crops only when it pleases him and it is no use for you plow your ground ... That is all wrong ...

Revival may be expected when Christian people confess and ask forgiveness for their sins ... Break up your fallow ground ... Stand up and let people know you stand for Jesus Christ ...

When may a revival he expected? ... When ... ministers ... thought they would die unless a revival would come to awaken their people, their students, their deacons, and their Sunday school workers, unless they would fall down on their faces and renounce the world and the works and deceits of the devil ...

A revival ... returns the church from her backsliding and ... causes the conversion of man and women; and it always includes the conviction of sin ... A revival helps to bring the unsaved to Jesus Christ.

Billy Sunday preached on prayer:

The man who truly prays "Thy kingdom come" cannot pass a saloon and not ask himself the question, "What can I do to get rid of that thing that is blighting the lives of thousands of young men, that is wrecking homes, and that is dragging men and women down to hell?"

You cannot pray "Thy kingdom come," and then rush to the polls and vote for the thing that is preventing that kingdom from coming. You cannot pray "Thy kingdom come" and then go and do the things that make the devil laugh.

For the man who truly prays "Thy kingdom come" it would be impossible to have one kind of religion on his knees and another when he is behind the counter; it would be impossible to have one kind of religion in the pew and another in politics. When a man truly prays "Thy kingdom come" he means it in everything or in nothing.

Billy Sunday's preaching against alcohol led to the passage of the 18th Amendment. He stated:

I am the sworn, eternal, uncompromising enemy of the Liquor Traffic. I ask no quarter and I give none. I have drawn the sword in defense of God, home, wife, children and native land, and I will never sheathe it until the undertaker pumps me full of embalming fluid, and if my wife is alive, I think I shall call her to my beside and say:

"Nell, when I am dead, send for the butcher and skin me, and have my hide tanned and made into drum heads, and hire men to go up and down the land and beat the drums and say, "My husband, 'Bill' Sunday still lives and gives the whiskey gang a run for its money."

In 1910, Billy Sunday preached a historic revival in Joplin, Missouri, a mining town known for hotels, women of the night, gambling and saloons. Rev. Frank Neff of the Independence Avenue Methodist Episcopal Church in Kansas City, and president of the Ministers Alliance of Joplin, told reporters:

> We expect a great clean up in the city, but it will be in the nature of a religious awakening which will result in a permanent clean up and will come from a sincere desire of the people.

During Joplin's "Fifty Days of Sunday," Billy Sunday explained:

> A revival is the conviction of sin. Inside the church there must be a spiritual revival before it gets outside.

In his animated style, Billy Sunday said:

> Temptation is the devil looking through the keyhole. Yielding is opening the door and inviting him in.

Billy Sunday warned not to remove the Bible from public schools:

> Rivers of America will run with blood filled to their banks before we will submit to them taking the Bible out of our schools.

His views were similar to Abraham Lincoln's, who, when presented with a Bible by a Colored Delegation from Baltimore, September 7, 1864, stated:

> In regard to this Great Book, I have but to say, it is the best gift God has given to men ... But for it we could not know right from wrong.

Billy Sunday inspired famous tent evangelists such as Billy Graham, T.L. Osborn, Oral

Roberts, and other revival preachers.

Speaking in city after city across America, tens of thousands heard him in month long meetings. Huge wooden auditoriums, called Billy Sunday Tabernacles, were built to accommodate the crowds.

The Billy Sunday Tabernacle in Winona was the largest auditorium in northern Indiana for many years, seating 7,500. A Billy Sunday museum is on the campus of Grace College and Seminary in Winona Lake, Indiana.

Billy Sunday was a pioneer in gospel radio broadcasting, along with:
• Paul Rader–pastor of Moody Church in Chicago;
• Charles Fuller–founder of Fuller Theological Seminary;
• Aimee Semple McPherson–founder of the Foursquare Church;
• William Ward Ayer–pastor of Calvary Baptist Church in Manhattan;
• Walter A. Maier–The Lutheran Hour;
• Donald Grey Barnhouse—The Bible Study Hour;
• "Fighting Bob" Shuler; and
• Father Charles Coughlin.

Religious radio stations were initially unregulated. Sometimes their powerful signals overlapped sports and other broadcasts, and occasionally they aired programing critical of politicians. This resulted in government regulating radio in 1926 by the FRC (Federal Radio Commission), which became the FCC in 1934.

In typical fashion, after the government began licensing, it began regulating, then revoking licenses, as it did to the popular radio broadcaster "Fighting Bob" Shuler in 1934, who was a national folk hero for exposing government corruption.

Billy Sunday taught that salvation was through faith in Jesus Christ, not in organized religion, explaining that churches were fine so far as they were "in the world, but all wrong when the world is in them," adding:

> You can go to hell just as fast from the church door as from the grog shop or bawdy house ... Going to church doesn't make you a Christian any more than going to a garage makes you an automobile.

He assured believers of God's forgiveness: "The devil says I'm out, but the Lord says I'm safe." He challenged:

> Live so that when the final summons comes you will leave something more behind you than an epitaph on a tombstone.

Billy Sunday stated:

> I never see a man or a woman or boy or girl but I do not think that God has a plan for them ... He will use each of us to His glory if we will only let Him.

CR

HELEN KELLER "THINGS UNSEEN ARE ETERNAL" "THINGS TO LEARN IN LIFE ... LOVE EVERYBODY SINCERELY ... TO TRUST GOD UNHESITATINGLY"

Helen Keller was born June 27, 1880. At the age of two she suffered an illness that left her blind and deaf. Her parents took her to Dr. Alexander Graham Bell who recommended the Perkins Institute for the Blind in Boston. It was there, at age of 7, that Helen was taught by Anne Sullivan through the sense of touch. Anne eventually taught her to read Braille.

Helen Keller began attending Radcliffe College, where Anne Sullivan interpreted the lectures. She became concerned about all the blind, especially those blinded in World War I or by poor working conditions. Though naive in her political views, she received numerous international honors for her efforts to help the blind.

Helen Keller learned to type on a Braille typewriter and wrote many books between 1903 and 1941, including: *The Story of My Life*, 1903; *Optimism*, 1903; *The World I Live In*, 1908; *The Song of the Stone Wall*, 1910; *Out of the Dark*, 1913; *My Religion*, 1927; *Midstream*, 1930; *Let Us Have Faith*, 1941; and *The Open Door*, 1957. She stated:

I thank God for my handicaps, for, through them, I have found myself, my work, and my God.

In the film documentary of her life, *The Unconquered,* Helen Keller responded to the question, "Can you see the world?":

> I can see, and that is why I can be so happy, in what you call the dark, but which to me is golden. I can see a God–made world, not a man–made world.

On June 26, 1955, regarding reading the Bible, Helen Keller stated:

> It gives me a deep comforting sense that "things seen are temporal and things unseen are eternal."

The Jewish and Christian view of the handicapped is different from other belief systems.

The traditional Islamic attitude is that a handicapped person is being punished or cursed of Allah. "Such are the men whom Allah has cursed for he has made them deaf and blinded their sight." (Qur'an 47:23) Hindu and Buddhist attitudes is that a handicapped person is being punished for sins of a supposed past life by an impersonal "bad" karma. The Socialist attitude is that a handicapped person is a burden on the State, being worth less because of their limited capacity to contribute to society.

The Jewish attitude is in:

> Leviticus 19:14: Thou shalt not curse the deaf, nor put a stumbling block before the blind, but shalt fear thy God: I am the LORD; and Deuteronomy 27:18: Cursed be he that maketh the blind to wander out of the way. And all the people shall say, Amen.

The Christian attitude was expressed by Jesus, who said:

Whatever you have done unto the least of these my brethren you have done unto me.

Helen Keller stated:

Just as all things upon earth represent and image forth all the realities of another world, so the Bible is one mighty representative of the whole spiritual life of humanity.

Helen Keller addressed the Lions Clubs International Foundation Convention in Cedar Point, Ohio, in 1925 on behalf of the American Foundation for the Blind:

Dear Lions and Ladies: I suppose you have heard the legend that represents opportunity as a capricious lady, who knocks at every door but once, and if the door isn't opened quickly, she passes on, never to return. And that is as it should be. Lovely, desirable ladies won't wait. You have to go out and grab 'em. I am your opportunity. I am knocking at your door. I want to be adopted ...

The American Foundation for the Blind ... grew out of the imperative needs of the blind ... Its object is to make the lives of the blind more worthwhile everywhere by increasing their economic value and giving them the joy of normal activity ...

Helen Keller continued:

Try to imagine how you would feel if you were suddenly stricken blind today. Picture yourself stumbling and groping at noonday as in the night; your work, your independence, gone. In that dark world, wouldn't you be glad if a friend took you by the hand and said, "Come with me and I will teach you how to do some of the things you used to do when you could see?"

That is just the kind of friend the American Foundation is going to be to all the blind in this country if seeing people will give it the support it must have.

You have heard how through a little word dropped from the fingers of another, a ray of light from another soul touched the darkness of my mind and I found myself, found the world, found God. It is because my teacher learned about me and broke through the dark, silent imprisonment which held me that I am able to work for myself and for others ...

She concluded:

It is the caring we want more than money. The gift without the sympathy and interest of the giver is empty. If you care, if we can make the people of this great country care, the blind will indeed triumph over blindness.

The opportunity I bring to you, Lions, is this: To foster and sponsor the work of the American Foundation for the Blind. Will you not help me hasten the day when there shall be no preventable blindness; no little deaf, blind child untaught; no blind man or woman unaided?

I appeal to you LIONS, you who have your sight, your hearing, you who are strong and brave and kind. Will you not constitute yourselves Knights of the Blind in this crusade against darkness? I thank you.

The LIONS adopted the mission for the detection of vision problems in children, provision of glasses for the needy, and many other projects, such as an initiative to eliminate river blindness in Africa.

The LIONS Eye Institution for Transplant and Research is the leading institution for ocular science. LIONS also supported the Vanderbilt Eye Center in Nashville, Tennessee.

On February 5, 1955, at age of 74, Helen Keller typed a message on a typewriter during an interview just before boarding an airplane for a 40,000 mile world–wide journey.

> It's wonderful to climb the liquid mountains of the sky. Behind me and before me is God and I have no fears.

On June 26, 1955, the day before her 75th birthday, Helen Keller stated: "Self–pity is our worst enemy and if we yield to it, we can never do anything wise in the world."

Helen Keller was introduced to President Grover Cleveland at age 7. She received letters from eight U.S. Presidents — from Theodore Roosevelt in 1903 to Lyndon B. Johnson in 1965. She met President Eisenhower in 1953, and President Kennedy in 1961.

She received the French Legion of Honor and the U.S. Presidential Medal of Freedom. On March 17, 2003, the U.S. Mint issued a quarter coin representing the State of Alabama which honored Helen Keller. A statue of Helen Keller as a young girl, learning the sense of touch at a water pump is in the U.S. Capitol from the State of Alabama.

Helen Keller concluded:

> Four things to learn in life: –To think clearly without hurry or confusion; –To love everybody sincerely; –To act in everything with the highest motives; –To trust God unhesitatingly.

ↄ⃝

EDDIE RICKENBACKER – WORLD WAR I FIGHTER ACE
"THANK GOD I HAVE CONTRIBUTED MY BEST TO THE LAND THAT CONTRIBUTED SO MUCH TO ME"

He began his career as an auto racer, gaining international fame by competing in the Indianapolis 500 four times, earning the nickname "Fast Eddie." When World War I started, he was sent to France in 1917, becoming the personal chauffeur driver of General John J. Pershing. His name was Edward Vernon "Eddie" Rickenbacker, born October 8, 1890.

During World War I, Germany's Red Baron was dominating the skies. Eddie Rickenbacker requested that he be transferred to the air service where he eventually became commanding officer of the 94th Aero Pursuit Squadron, with its famous "Hat–in–the–Ring" insignia.

This Squadron was responsible for destroying 69 enemy aircraft, the highest number shot down by any American Squadron. Flying over 300 combat hours, Rickenbacker personally shot down 26 enemy aircraft. He was awarded the Medal of Honor by President Herbert Hoover in 1931.

He wrote his World War I experiences in the book, *Fighting the Flying Circus,* 1919, such as one story:

> ... three–quarters of an hour of gasoline remained ... and no compass. Then I thought of the north star! Glory be! There she shines! I had been going west instead of south ... Keeping the star behind my rudder I flew south for fifteen minutes, then ... found myself above ... the River Meuse ... picked up our faithful searchlight and ten minutes later I landed ...

> As I walked across the field to my bed I looked up ... and repeated most fervently, "Thank God!"

Eddie Rickenbacker wrote of the courage of fellow pilot Lt. Quentin Roosevelt, the son of President Theodore Roosevelt:

> Quentin flew about alone for a while, then discovering, as he supposed, his own formation ahead of him he overtook them, dropped in behind ... To his horror he discovered that he had been following an enemy patrol all the time! Every machine ahead of him wore a huge black maltese cross on its wings and tail! ... Quentin fired one long burst ...

> The aeroplane immediately preceding him dropped at once and within a second or two burst into flames. Quentin put down his nose and streaked it for home before the astonished Huns had time to notice what had happened.

Quentin was shot down in a dogfight, July 14, 1918, as Rickenbacker wrote: "Quentin Roosevelt's death was a sad blow to the whole group."

In recounting barely escaping death himself, Eddie Rickenbacker wrote:

I want to make it clear that this escape and the others were not the result of any super ability or knowledge on my part. I wouldn't be alive today if I had to depend on that. I realized then, as I headed for France on one wing, that there had to be something else.

I had seen others die, brighter and more able than I. I knew there was a power. I believe in calling upon it for aid and for guidance. I am not such an egotist as to believe that God has spared me because I am I. I believe there is work for me to do and that I am spared to do it, just as you are.

After World War I, Rickenbacker started an automobile company – the Rickenbacker Motor Company, including technological innovations such as the first four–wheel brake system.

In 1925, in a highly publicized case, he supported General Billy Mitchell, who was court–martialed for criticizing the military's failure to upgrade their airplanes. Gary Cooper starred in a 1955 movie distributed by Warner Brothers, titled *The Court–Martial of Billy Mitchell.*

In 1927, he became owner of the Indianapolis Speedway, famous for its annual 500 mile auto race. Eddie Rickenbacker worked for Eastern Airlines, and eventually bought it.

He opposed President Franklin Roosevelt's New Deal policies as creating a "socialized welfare state," which drew criticism from the liberal media. Roosevelt's administration even ordered NBC Radio not to broadcast Rickenbacker's remarks.

Rickenbacker gave an hour–long speech at the Chicago Economic Club, April 1961, titled "Conservatives Must Face Up to Liberalism," which was reprinted by the thousands as a pamphlet. In it, he stated that America's Founding Fathers were:

> ... liberals in the true freedom–loving sense of the word ... In their zeal for liberty they feared the powers of government ... Government is like fire: a dangerous servant and a fearful master ... (It needs) limits, checks, balances, and control ...

> By some queer twist of language, the modern liberals are those who ceaselessly strive to pile up the power of government ... They systematically depleted the most precious resource in this nation's inheritance, namely, American freedom ...

Rickenbacker added:

> Freedom is not a physical object. It is a spiritual and a moral environment ... The evil of liberalism is its emphasis on material things and its disdain for the spiritual and moral resources that we call liberty.

> The liberal would sweep aside the constitutional restraints upon government in a blind rush to supply food, clothes, houses and financial security from birth to death, from the cradle to the grave for everybody.

He explained that liberals view people collectively, while "... the conservative knows that to regard man of a part of an undifferentiated mass is to consign him to ultimate slavery."

In his address titled "Americanism versus Communism," November 1, 1971, Rickenbacker warned:

> A government that is large enough to give you all you want is large enough to

take all you own first.

In 1942, Secretary of War Henry L. Stimson asked Rickenbacker to go on a special mission to the Pacific to inspect the military bases. Flying from Hawaii to New Guinea to meet with General Douglas MacArthur, the plane's inadequate navigational equipment resulted in them being hundreds of miles off–course. Out of fuel, the plane ditched in the ocean, October 21, 1942.

For 24 days, in almost hopeless conditions, Eddie Rickenbacker and seven others drifted aimlessly on the open sea. Lt. James Whittaker described in his book, *We Thought We Heard The Angels Sing* (1943), that they shivered wet all night but baked in the burning sun all day, and fought off sharks:

> Those giant swells hadn't looked so bad from high in the air, but down among them they were mountainous ... Rick maintained with a perfectly straight face that he was not in the least upset ...

> A swift movement beside our raft caught my eye and I turned ... The water about the raft fleet was alive with the triangular, dorsal fins of sharks.

The crew would have given up had not 52-year-old Eddie Rickenbacker, the oldest person on the raft, continued to encourage them. Lt. James Whittaker wrote:

> Col. James C. Adamson ... suddenly raised himself over the side of the raft and slid into the water. Quick as a flash, Rick had him. We hurriedly pulled the rafts in close and helped push the Colonel back into his boat ... Rick took over.

I will not put down all the things he said. They would scorch this paper. But from then on, woe betide the man who appeared about to turn quitter ... That man Rickenbacker has got a rough tongue in his head.

Lt. James Whittaker continued:

At length Private Johnny Bartek got out his Testament and by common consent we pulled the rafts together for a prayer meeting. We said the Lord's prayer ...

I didn't have the least notion that this open–air hallelujah meeting was going to do any good ... I observed that Rick seemed to encourage the suggestion and appeared inclined to take part ...

Col. Adamson was reading from the Testament. Suddenly Cherry stopped him. "What was that last, Colonel?" he demanded. "Where is that from?"

"It is from the Gospel According to Matthew," Col. Adamson replied. "Do you like it?" "It's the best thing I've heard yet. Read it again, Colonel."

Col. Adamson then read from the 31st through the 34th verses of the sixth chapter of Matthew: "Therefore, take ye no thought, saying: What shall we eat? or What shall we drink? or, Wherewithal shall we be clothed? For these are things the heathen seeketh. For your Heavenly Father knoweth that ye have need of all these things.

But seek ye first the kingdom of God, and His righteousness; and all these things shall be added unto you. Take therefore no thought for the morrow; for the morrow shall take thought for the things of itself. Each day has enough trouble of its own."

Lt. James Whittaker continued:

>I was somewhat impressed and said so. Then I was a little surprised at myself and added that the evil certainly had been sufficient unto the last two or three days ...

>I thought of these words during the wet, dreary night that followed. I dismissed them finally with the decision I would believe when I saw the food and drink. I was destined to see something startlingly like proof the following night.

Flight Engineer Private Johnny Bartek of Freehold, N.J., wrote in his book, *Life Out There* (1943) that on the 8th day, after reading from the Bible, Matthew 6:31–34, a sea gull landed on Rickenbacker's head:

>... but as we went on we all began to believe in the Bible and God and prayer ... We prayed and prayed for the sea gull to land so we could catch him ... After reading the passage, about twenty minutes later, that's when the sea gull landed on Eddie Rickenbacker's head.

Rickenbacker caught it and they used it for food and fish bait, with a fishhook made from a bent key ring. Succumbing to exposure and dehydration, Lt. James Whittaker wrote further in *We Thought We Heard The Angels Sing* (1943):

>We said the Lord's prayer again ... While we rolled and wallowed over the crests and into the troughs I was thinking that this was God's chance to make a believer of Jim Whittaker ...

>Eventually I became aware something was tugging insistently at my consciousness.

I looked over to the left. A cloud that had been fleecy and white a while ago now was darkening by the second.

While I watched, a bluish curtain unrolled from the cloud to the sea. It was rain – and moving toward us! Now everyone saw the downpour, sweeping across the ocean and speckling the waves with giant drops.

"Here she is!" Cherry shouted. "Thanks, Old Master!" Another minute and we were being deluged by sheets of cold water that splashed into our parched mouths and sluiced the caked salt off our burned and stinging bodies. We cupped our hands to guide the life–giving rivulets down our throats ...

We soaked and wrung out our shirts until all the salt was washed out of them. Then we saturated them again and wrung the water into our mouths.

Eddie Rickenbacker described their survival in his book, *Seven Came Through* (1943). Regarding America, Eddie Rickenbacker wrote:

I pray to God every night of my life to be given the strength and power to continue my efforts to inspire in others the interest, the obligation and the responsibilities that we owe to this land for the sake of future generations – for my boys and girls – so that we can always look back when the candle of life burns low and say, "Thank God I have contributed my best to the land that contributed so much to me."

Rickenbacker gave generously to: Army Air Forces Aid Society, Children's Village of Dobbs Ferry, Boys Athletic League, Big Brothers, Gramercy Boys Club, Boys Club of New

226   *MIRACLES IN AMERICAN HISTORY - VOLUME TWO: AMAZING FAITH THAT SHAPED THE NATION - SUSIE FEDERER*

York, Madison Square Boys Club, Boys Club of America, and the Boy Scouts of America, as it emphasized "duty to God & Country" and being "morally straight."

He donated his Bear Creek Ranch in Texas to the Boy Scouts in 1957. He confided:

> It was clear to me that God had a purpose in keeping me alive ... I had been saved to serve.

Columnist Ray Tucker wrote "Rickenbacker has become an evangelist without knowing it. There is an unworldly gleam in his eyes and a quaver in his voice these days."

In 1943, Rickenbacker wrote an article "When a Man Faces Death," published in *The American Magazine,* stating: "The easiest thing in the world is to die. The hardest is to live."

Eddie died July 23, 1973. Jimmy Dolittle, of the famous Dolittle's Raiders, spoke at his memorial service at Key Biscayne Presbyterian Church.

In the book *Eddie Rickenbacker–An American Hero in the Twentieth Century* (Baltimore, MD: The John Hopkins University Press, 2005), author W. David Lewis described responses to Rickenbacker's national radio broadcasts, such as a letter from listeners in California:

> We listened to your radio broadcasts and now we know why you were saved, as we have needed someone in this good country of ours who was not afraid to speak their convictions ... The history of our country shows that in every crisis God has always produced a man strong enough for the time and we feel strongly that you were the man for this time.

THE WHITE HOUSE
WASHINGTON

As Commander-in-Chief I
take pleasure in commending
the reading of the Bible to
all who serve in the armed
forces of the United States.
Throughout the centuries
men of many faiths and
diverse origins have found
in the Sacred Book words
of wisdom, counsel and
inspiration. It is a fountain of strength and now,
as always, an aid in attain-
ing the highest aspirations
of the human soul.

CR

U.S. MILITARY: *"FOR GOD & COUNTRY"*

Yale President Ezra Stiles addressed Connecticut's General Assembly, May 8, 1783, regarding General George Washington being chosen to command the Continental Army:

> The memorable battle of Bunker Hill (June 17, 1775) ... convinced us ... that Americans both would and could fight with great effect. Whereupon Congress put at the head of this spirited army, the only man (George Washington), on whom the eyes of all Israel were placed ...

> This American JOSHUA was raised up by God, and divinely formed by a peculiar influence of the Sovereign of the Universe, for the great work of leading the armies ... to liberty and independence ...

Stiles continued:

> And while we render our supreme honors to the Most High, the God of armies; let us recollect, with affectionate honor, the bold and brave sons of freedom, who willingly offered themselves, and bled in the defense of their country ...

> The officers and soldiers of the patriot army ... and ... gallant commanders and brave seamen of the American navy, have heroically fought the war by sea and by

land ... Never was the profession of arms used with more glory, in a better cause, since the days of JOSHUA, the son of Nun.

After having the Declaration of Independence read to his troops, General George Washington issued the order, July 9, 1776:

> Commanding officers of each regiment are directed to procure Chaplains ... persons of good Characters and exemplary lives – To see that all inferior officers and soldiers pay them a suitable respect and attend carefully upon religious exercises.

> The blessing and protection of Heaven are at all times necessary but especially so in times of public distress and danger –

> The General hopes and trusts, that every officer and man, will endeavor so to live, and act, as becomes a Christian Soldier, defending the dearest Rights and Liberties of his country ... The peace and safety of his Country depends, under God, solely on the success of our arms.

On May 2, 1778, General George Washington issued the order to his troops at Valley Forge:

> The Commander-in-Chief directs that Divine service be performed every Sunday at 11 o'clock, in each Brigade which has a Chaplain. Those Brigades which have none will attend the places of worship nearest to them. It is expected that officers of all ranks will, by their attendance, set an example for their men.

> While we are zealously performing the duties of good citizens and soldiers,

we certainly ought not to be inattentive to the higher duties of religion. To the distinguished character of Patriot, it should be our highest Glory to laud the more distinguished Character of Christian.

On November 15, 1862, President Abraham Lincoln ordered:

The discipline and character of the national forces should not suffer nor the cause they defend be imperiled by the profanation of the day or name of the Most High ...

"At this time of public distress," adopting the words of Washington in 1776, "men may find enough to do in the service of God and their country without abandoning themselves to vice and immorality ..."

Lincoln added:

The first general order issued by the Father of his Country after the Declaration of Independence indicates the spirit in which our institutions were founded and should ever be defended:

"The General hopes and trusts that every officer and man will endeavor to live and act as becomes a Christian soldier defending the dearest rights and liberties of his country."

President Benjamin Harrison ordered, June 7, 1889:

In November, 1862, President Lincoln quoted the words of Washington to sustain his own views, and announced in a general order that –

"The President, Commander-in-Chief of the Army and Navy, desires and enjoins the orderly observance of the Sabbath by the officers and men in the military and naval service. The importance for man and beast of the prescribed weekly rest, the sacred rights of Christian soldiers and sailors, a becoming deference to the best sentiment of a Christian people, and a due regard for the Divine Will demand that Sunday labor in the Army and Navy be reduced to the measure of strict necessity" ...

President Harrison added:

... To recall the kindly and considerate spirit of the orders issued by these great men in the most trying times of our history, and to promote contentment and efficiency, the President directs that Sunday morning inspection will be merely of the dress and general appearance.

President Woodrow Wilson gave the order, January 20, 1918:

The President, Commander-in-Chief of the Army and Navy, following the reverent example of his predecessors, desires and enjoins the orderly observance of the Sabbath by the officers and men in the military and naval service of the United States.

The importance for man and beast of the prescribed weekly rest, the sacred rights of Christian soldiers and sailors, a becoming deference to the best sentiment of a Christian people, and a due regard for the Divine Will demand that Sunday labor in the Army and Navy be reduced to the measure of strict necessity.

Such an observance of Sunday is dictated by the best traditions of our people and by the convictions of all who look to Divine Providence for guidance and protection, and, in repeating in this order the language of President Lincoln, the President is confident that he is speaking alike to the hearts and to the consciences of those under his authority.

In 1917, President Woodrow Wilson wrote the foreword to a pocket Bible given out by the thousands to American soldiers heading to France and Belgium during World War I:

> The Bible is the Word of Life. I beg that you will read it and find this out for yourselves ... When you have read the Bible you will know it is the Word of God, because you will have found in it the key to your own heart ... –(signed) Woodrow Wilson.

General John J. Pershing wrote a Preface of the New Testament & Book of Psalms, August 10, 1917:

> To the American Soldier aroused against a nation waging war in violation of all Christian principles ... Hardships will be your lot, but trust in God will give you comfort; temptation will befall you, but the teachings of our Savior will give you strength. –(signed) Pershing, Comdg.

In 1917, former President Theodore Roosevelt inscribed the foreword to a pocket New Testament & Psalms given to World War I soldiers, published by the New York Bible Society:

> The teachings of the New Testament are foreshadowed in Micah's verse (Micah 6: 8): "What more does the Lord require of thee than to do justice, and to love mercy,

and to walk humbly with thy God?"

Do Justice; and therefore fight valiantly against the armies of Germany and Turkey, for these nations in this crisis stand for the reign of Moloch and Beelzebub on this earth. –(signed) Theodore Roosevelt.

At the beginning of World War II, on January 25, 1941, President Franklin D. Roosevelt wrote the prologue of a special Gideons' edition of the New Testament & Book of Psalms distributed to millions of soldiers:

As Commander-in-Chief, I take pleasure in commending the reading of the Bible to all who serve in the armed forces of the United States ... –(signed) Franklin D. Roosevelt.

In December 1944, during the Battle of the Bulge, General George M. Patton had Chaplain Fr. James O'Neil compose a prayer. It was printed on a quarter of a million cards and distributed to the soldiers of the Third Army:

Almighty and most merciful Father, we humbly beseech Thee, of Thy great goodness, to restrain these immoderate rains with which we have had to contend. Grant us fair weather for Battle. Graciously hearken to us as soldiers who call Thee that, armed with Thy power, we may advance from victory to victory, and crush the oppression and wickedness of our enemies, and establish Thy justice among men and nations. Amen.

Five Star General Douglas MacArthur, who was the Supreme Commander of Allied

Forces in the Southwest Pacific during World War II, told West Point cadets, May 1962:

> The soldier, above all other men, is required to practice the greatest act of religious training–sacrifice. In battle and in the face of danger and death, he discloses those Divine attributes which his Maker gave when He created man in His own image ...

> No physical courage and no brute instinct can take the place of Divine help which alone can sustain him. However horrible the incidents of war may be, the soldier who is called upon to offer and to give his life for his country is the noblest development of mankind.

In 1947, the U.S. Corp of Cadets required:

> Attendance at chapel is part of a cadet's training; no cadet will be exempted. Each cadet will receive religious training in one of the three particular faiths: Protestant, Catholic or Jewish.

In 1949, the U.S. Naval Academy required:

> All Midshipmen, except those on authorized outside church parties, shall attend Sunday services in the chapel.

On August 17, 1955, President Dwight Eisenhower, who had served as Supreme Commander Allied Expeditionary Forces during World War II, authorized the code of conduct for U.S. soldiers, which stated:

> I serve in the forces which guard my country and our way of life. I am prepared to give my life in their defense ... If captured ... I will accept neither parole nor

special favors from the enemy ... I will never forget I am an American fighting man, responsible for my actions and dedicated to the principles which made my country free. I will trust in my God and in the United States of America.

The Missing Man Table to remember Prisoners of War has traditionally had a Bible placed on it, to represent the strength gained through faith to sustain those lost from our country, founded as one nation under God.

President Dwight Eisenhower stated December 24, 1953, lighting the National Christmas Tree:

> George Washington long ago rejected exclusive dependence upon mere materialistic values. In the bitter and critical winter at Valley Forge, when the cause of liberty was so near defeat, his recourse was sincere and earnest prayer ... As religious faith is the foundation of free government, so is prayer an indispensable part of that faith.

President Eisenhower broadcast from the White House for the American Legion's Back–to–God Program, February 7, 1954:

> As a former soldier, I am delighted that our veterans are sponsoring a movement to increase our awareness of God in our daily lives. In battle, they learned a great truth – that there are no atheists in the foxholes. They know that in time of test and trial, we instinctively turn to God for new courage.

President Dwight Eisenhower stated at the opening of the White House Conference of Mayors, December 14, 1953:

I want to point out something about fighting – about war ... The winning of war – the effectiveness in such things – is in the heart, in the determination, in the faith. It is in our belief in our country, in our God, everything that goes to make up America.

President Eisenhower, February 20, 1955, stated for the American Legion Back–To–God Program:

The Founding Fathers ... recognizing God as the author of individual rights, declared that the purpose of Government is to secure those rights ... But in many lands the State claims to be the author of human rights ... If the State gives rights, it can – and inevitably will – take away those rights.

Without God, there could be no American form of Government, nor an American way of life. Recognition of the Supreme Being is the first – the most basic – expression of Americanism.

Thus the Founding Fathers saw it, and thus, with God's help, it will continue to be ... Veterans realize, perhaps more clearly than others, the prior place that Almighty God holds in our national life.

FOUR CHAPLAINS DAY – "TODAY AS THEN, THERE IS NEED FOR ... RENEWED RECOGNITION THAT FAITH IS OUR SUREST STRENGTH, OUR GREATEST RESOURCE"

On the frigid night of February 3, 1943, the overcrowded Allied ship *U.S.A.T. Dorchester,* carrying 902 servicemen, plowed through the dark waters near Greenland.

At 1:00am, a Nazi submarine fired a torpedo into the transport's flank, killing many in the explosion and trapping others below deck. It sank in 27 minutes.

The two escort ships, Coast Guard cutters *Comanche* and *Escanaba,* were able to rescue only 231 survivors. In the chaos of fire, smoke, oil and ammonia, four chaplains calmed sailors and distributed life jackets: Lt. George L. Fox, Methodist; Lt. Clark V. Poling, Dutch Reformed; Lt. John P. Washington, Roman Catholic; and Lt. Alexander D. Goode, Jewish.

When there were no more life jackets, the four chaplains ripped off their own and put them on four young men. As the ship went down, survivors floating in rafts could see the four chaplains linking arms and bracing themselves on the slanting deck. They bowed their heads in prayer as they sank to their icy deaths.

Survivor Grady Clark wrote:

As I swam away from the ship, I looked back. The flares had lighted everything. The bow came up high and she slid under. The last thing I saw, the Four Chaplains were up there praying for the safety of the men. They had done everything they could. I did not see them again. They themselves did not have a chance without their life jackets.

In 1998, Congress honored them by declaring February 3rd "Four Chaplains Day." President Franklin D. Roosevelt acknowledged Protestants, Catholics, and Jews working together for liberty in his address at Madison Square Garden, October 28, 1940:

> Your government is working ... with representatives of Catholic, Protestant, and Jewish faiths. Without these three, all three of them ... things would not be as ... easy.

FDR stated January 31, 1938:

> There has been definite progress towards a spiritual reawakening ... I receive evidences of this from all our Protestant Churches; I get it from Catholic priests and from Jewish rabbis as well.

FDR stated December 6, 1933:

> Government guarantees to the churches — Gentile and Jewish — the right to worship God in their own way.

In a Radio Address, November 4, 1940, FDR stated:

> Democracy is the birthright of every citizen, the white and the colored; the Protestant, the Catholic, the Jew.

On February 3, 1951, President Harry S. Truman dedicated the Chapel of the Four Chaplains, currently located at the Philadelphia Naval Shipyard. Truman said:

> This interfaith shrine ... will stand through long generations to teach Americans that as men can die heroically as brothers so should they live together in mutual faith and goodwill.

On February 7, 1954, President Dwight Eisenhower spoke from the White House for the American Legion "Back–to–God" Program:

> And we remember that, only a decade ago, aboard the transport *Dorchester,* four chaplains of four faiths together willingly sacrificed their lives so that four others might live ...

Eisenhower continued:

> Today as then, there is need for positive acts of renewed recognition that faith is our surest strength, our greatest resource. This "Back to God" movement is such a positive act ... Whatever our individual church, whatever our personal creed, our common faith in God is a common bond among us ...

> Together we thank the Power that has made and preserved us a nation. By the millions, we speak prayers, we sing hymns–and no matter what their words may be, their spirit is the same – "In God is Our Trust."

In 1984, the Chapel of the Four Chaplains gave an award recognizing the military chaplain team, made up of a Protestant minister, a Catholic priest, and a Jewish rabbi, who were present at the 1983 Beirut Bombing where fundamental Islamic terrorists blew up the U.S. Marine barracks, killing 241 U.S. Marines. President Ronald Reagan memorialized them in a speech at the Baptist Annual Convention, April 13, 1984:

> On that October day when a terrorist truck bomb took the lives of 241 marines, soldiers, and sailors at the airport in Beirut, one of the first to reach the tragic scene was a chaplain, the chaplain of our 6th Fleet, Rabbi Arnold E. Resnicoff ...

> He said, "Screams of those injured or trapped were barely audible at first, as our minds struggled to grapple with the reality before us – a massive four–story building, reduced to a pile of rubble; dust mixing with smoke and fire, obscuring our view of the little that was left ...

> Trying to pull and carry those whose injuries appeared less dangerous in an immediate sense than the approaching fire or the smothering smoke–my kippa was lost. (That is the little headgear that is worn by rabbis.)

> The last I remember it, I'd used it to mop someone's brow. Father Pucciarelli, the Catholic chaplain, cut a circle out of his cap – a piece of camouflaged cloth which would become my temporary head–covering. Somehow he wanted those marines to know not just that we were chaplains, but that he was a Christian and that I was Jewish ..."

Reagan continued quoting Chaplain Rabbi Resnicoff:

> The words from the prophet Malachi kept recurring to me – words he'd uttered

some 2,500 years ago as he had looked around at fighting and cruelty and pain. "Have we not all one Father?" he had asked. "Has not one God created us all?" ...

To understand the role of the chaplain – Jewish, Catholic, or Protestant – is to understand that we try to remind others, and perhaps ourselves as well, to cling to our humanity even in the worst of times ...

We bring with us the truth that faith not only reminds us of the holy in Heaven, but also of the holiness we can create here on Earth ... We have within us the power to reflect as God's creatures the highest values of our Creator. As God is forgiving and – merciful, so can we be."

Reagan stated January 31, 1983:

Let us come together, Christians and Jews, let us pray together ... All of us, as Protestants, Catholics, and Jews, have a special responsibility to remember our fellow believers who are being persecuted in other lands. We're all children of Abraham. We're children of the same God.

Another inspiring story of a Christian risking his life to save soldiers was combat medic Desmond Doss, as portrayed in the award–winning film *Hacksaw Ridge* (2016).

Yet another inspiring story was that of Chaplain William Thomas Cummings, who served with the U.S. Army in the Philippines during World War II. He was captured by the Japanese and died when his unmarked prisoner ship was sunk sailing to Japan on January 18, 1945.

Earlier, while serving with the American troops during the Battle of Bataan, January 7 to April 9, 1942, Chaplain Father Cummings gave a stirring field sermon in which he declared: "There are no atheists in the foxholes."

On February 7, 1954, President Dwight Eisenhower spoke from the White House for the American Legion "Back–to–God" Program:

> As a former soldier, I am delighted that our veterans are sponsoring a movement to increase our awareness of God in our daily lives. In battle, they learned a great truth – that there are no atheists in the foxholes.
>
> They know that in time of test and trial, we instinctively turn to God for new courage and peace of mind. All the history of America bears witness to this truth ...
>
> In the three centuries that separate the Pilgrims of the *Mayflower* from the chaplains of the *Dorchester,* America's freedom, her courage, her strength, and her progress have had their foundation in faith.

CR

JOHN F. KENNEDY & PT109 – "LET US ... LEAD THE LAND WE LOVE, ASKING HIS BLESSING & HIS HELP, KNOWING THAT HERE ON EARTH GOD'S WORK MUST TRULY BE OUR OWN"

The South Pacific had many major battles during World War II:
- Pearl Harbor, Dec. 7, 1941; • Wake Island, Dec. 7–23, 1941;
- Doolittle Raid, April 18, 1942; • Coral Sea, May 4–8, 1942;
- Midway, June 4–7, 1942; • Guadalcanal campaign, Aug. 7, 1942–Feb. 9, 1943;
- Gilbert & Marshall Islands campaign, 1943–44: Makin Island, Aug. 17–18, 1942; Tarawa, Nov. 20, 1943; Makin, Nov. 20–23, 1943; Kwajalein, Feb. 14, 1944; Eniwetok, Feb. 17, 1944[
- Truk Island, Feb. 17–18, 1944; • Mariana & Palau Islands campaign 1944: Saipan, June 16, 1944; Philippine Sea, June 19–20, 1944; Guam, July 21, 1944; Tinian, July 24, 1944; Peleliu, Sept. 15, 1944; Angaur, Sept. 17, 1944;
- Leyte & Leyte Gulf, Oct. 23–29, 1944; • Iwo Jima, Feb. 19, 1945;
- Okinawa, April 1, 1945.

After the Guadalcanal campaign, which was the Allied forces first major offensive, the U.S. began island hopping, securing the Solomon Islands.

Lieutenant John F. Kennedy commanded the *PT–109*, one of the small 80 foot–long Navy patrol torpedo boats used to monitor and disrupt the Tokyo Express – the shipping lanes used by Imperial Japan's destroyers through the Ferguson and Blackett Straits.

PT boats operated almost exclusively at night, often in fog and without reliable radar. They fired their torpedoes at close range, then sped away.

On the foggy night of August, 2, 1943, PT–109 was idling on one engine to avoid detection while awaiting approaching enemy destroyers. The crew was shocked to realize they were in the direct path of an oncoming speeding destroyer, the *Amagiri*. With just seconds to respond, they were unable to avoid collision. The *PT–109* was rammed, broken in half, and began to sink.

After the war, author Robert Donovan interviewed crew members of the *Amagiri* and concluded that the destroyer intentionally rammed the *PT–109*. In May of 2002, a National Geographic Society expedition, headed by Robert Ballard, found the wreckage of the *PT–109*.

Though sustaining permanent back injuries, Kennedy, who had been on Harvard's swim team, helped the 11 survivors swim to shore. Since Imperial Japanese occupied the larger islands, he chose for them to swim 3.5 miles to the small, uninhabited Plum Pudding Island, which was only 100 yards wide.

They swam for four hours, with Kennedy towing in his clenched teeth the life–jacket strap of the ship's injured machinist, Patrick MacMahon. Hiding from passing Japanese barges, they realized there was no food or water on the island.

That night, Kennedy swam 2 miles to Ferguson Passage hoping to flag down a passing PT boat. Unsuccessful, he swam to islands Olasana, then Nauro, before returning to Plum Pudding Island. Kennedy convinced his crew they had to swim to Olasana Island.

On August 4, Kennedy and Lenny Thom helped the dehydrated, starving, and injured crew swim 2 miles to Olasana Island, where there was a small amount of water and a few coconuts. An Australian coastwatcher asked some friendly islanders to search for them, which was a risky request, as other islanders who had been caught helping Americans were tortured and killed.

Initially they mistook Kennedy, who had swum back to Nauro to scavenge, as being Japanese, as the one islander commented "All white people looked the same to me." The islanders then paddled 35 miles back to the American base at Rendova Island, carrying a coconut, in which Kennedy carved the message:

NAURO ISL, COMMANDER ... NATIVE KNOWS POS'IT ... HE CAN
PILOT... 11 ALIVE NEED SMALL BOAT... KENNEDY.

On August 8, Lieutenant William Liebenow on the *PT–157* came to rescue them. The arranged signal for the pickup was for Kennedy to fire four shots. As he only had three bullets in his pistol, a discarded Japanese rifle was used to shoot the fourth. Once safely on the *PT–157,* the rescued crew sang "Yes Jesus Loves Me."

For his part, Kennedy was awarded the Navy and Marine Corp Medal for heroism. In 1963, Cliff Robertson starred as Kennedy in the movie *PT–109.* It was the first movie about a sitting President released while he was still in office.

Unfortunately, one of Kennedy's brothers, Joseph, Jr., was killed in World War II in Europe. John F. Kennedy went on to become a U.S. Congressman and a U.S. Senator.

Kennedy defeated Vice-President Richard Nixon in one of the closest Presidential elections in U.S. history – by 0.2 percent, a mere 118,000 votes out of 69 million. After swearing in as the 35th President, John F. Kennedy stated in his Inaugural Address:

> I have sworn before you and Almighty God the same solemn oath our forbears prescribed nearly a century and three-quarters ago ... yet the same revolutionary beliefs for which our forebears fought are still at issue around the globe—the belief that the rights of man come not from the generosity of the state but from the hand of God ...

> Let us go forth to lead the land we love, asking His blessing and His help, but knowing that here on earth God's work must truly be our own.

In the White House Rose Garden, November 21, 1961, John F. Kennedy said:

> When we all – regardless of our particular religious convictions – draw our guidance and inspiration, and really, in a sense, moral direction, from the same general area, the Bible, the Old and the New Testaments, we have every reason to

believe that our various religious denominations should live together in the closest harmony ...

He concluded:

The basic presumption of the moral law, the existence of God, man's relationship to Him – there is generally consensus on those questions.

Kennedy told the Zionists of America Convention at the Statler Hilton Hotel in New York, August 26, 1960:

When the first Zionist conference met in 1897, Palestine was a neglected wasteland. A few scattered Jewish colonies had resettled there ... Most of the governments of the world were indifferent. But now all is changed. Israel became a triumphant and enduring reality exactly 50 years after Theodore Herzl, the prophet of Zionism, had proclaimed the ideal of nationhood ...

He continued:

Herzl was then only 37 years of age ... Jewish people – ever since David slew Goliath – have never considered youth as a barrier to leadership ...

I first saw Palestine in 1939. There the neglect and ruin left by centuries of Ottoman misrule were slowly being transformed by miracles of labor and sacrifice ... I returned in 1951 to see the grandeur of Israel. In 3 years this new state had opened its doors to 600,000 immigrants and refugees. Even while fighting for its own survival, Israel had given new hope to the persecuted and new dignity to the pattern of Jewish life.

I left with the conviction that the United Nations may have conferred on Israel the credentials of nationhood; but its own idealism and courage, its own sacrifice and generosity, had earned the credentials of immortality ...

Kennedy added:

Israel is here to stay. For Israel was not created in order to disappear – Israel will endure and flourish. It is the child of hope and the home of the brave. It can neither be broken by adversity nor demoralized by success. It carries the shield of democracy and it honors the sword of freedom ... Israel is a cause that stands beyond the ordinary changes and chances of American public life ...

There is a special obligation on the Democratic Party. It was President Woodrow Wilson who forecast with prophetic wisdom the creation of a Jewish homeland.

It was President Franklin Roosevelt who kept alive the hopes of Jewish redemption during the Nazi terror. It was President Harry Truman who first recognized the new State of Israel and gave it status in world affairs. And may I add that it would be my hope and my pledge to continue this Democratic tradition – and to be worthy of it ...

Kennedy concluded:

When I talked with Prime Minister Ben–Gurion on his most recent visit to this country, he told me of dangerous signs of unrest beneath the deceptive quiet that has fallen over the Middle East. For there is no peace in that region ...

The Arab peoples rose to ... independence in the very years which saw the rise of Israel ... But from their destructive vendetta can come nothing but misery and poverty and the risk of war ... The Middle East needs water, not war ...

Ancient rivers would give their power to new industries. The desert would yield to civilization. Disease would be eradicated, especially the disease that strikes down helpless children. The blight of poverty would be replaced by the blessings of abundance ... "Seek peace, and pursue it" commands the psalmist.

Iran was considered the most pro–American nation in the Middle East until abandoned by President Jimmy Carter. In April of 1962, President John F. Kennedy and First Lady Jacqueline welcomed Shah Reza Pahlavi and Empress Farah to the White House. Kennedy stated:

Your majesty, I speak on behalf of all of my fellow Americans in welcoming you to the United States. The interest of the both of us is the same: to maintain our freedom, to maintain our peace, and to provide a better life for our people.

At the Presidential Prayer Breakfast, February 9, 1961, President John F. Kennedy stated:

This country was founded by men and women ... dedicated to two propositions: FIRST, a strong religious conviction, and SECONDLY a recognition that this conviction could flourish only under a system of freedom ...

Kennedy continued:

The Puritans and the Pilgrims of my own section of New England, the Quakers of Pennsylvania, the Catholics of Maryland, the Presbyterians of North Carolina, the

Methodists and Baptists who came later, all shared these two great traditions which, like silver threads, have run through the warp and the woof of American history ...

He added:

Let us go forth to lead this land that we love, joining in the prayer of General George Washington in 1783,

"that God would have you in His holy protection ... that He would most graciously be pleased to dispose us all to do justice, to love mercy, and to demean ourselves with ... the characteristics of the Divine Author of our blessed religion, without an humble imitation of whose example we can never hope to be a happy nation ..."

President Kennedy concluded:

The guiding principle and prayer of this Nation has been, is now, and ever shall be "In God We Trust."

Commander Mitsuo Fuchida training for the Pearl Harbor attack, October 1941

Send the message: "Tora! Tora! Tora!"

from "PEARL HARBOR TO GOLGOTHA"

MITSUO FUCHIDA

CR

GOD'S SAMURAI – LEAD PILOT AT PEARL HARBOR BECOMES CHRISTIAN EVANGELIST: MITSUO FUCHIDA

Mitsuo Fuchida was the Imperial Japanese Navy pilot who led the attack on Pearl Harbor, shouting, "Tora, Tora, Tora." In 1950, he became a Christian, then an evangelist, and then in 1960, an American citizen.

Fuchida was depicted in the 1970 Movie *Tora, Tora, Tora*. His story was written in *Readers Digest* "God's Samurai: Lead Pilot at Pearl Harbor" (February 1954).

Mitsuo Fuchida wrote in *From Pearl Harbor to Calvary* (1953):

> I was in Hiroshima the day before the atom bomb was dropped ... Fortunately, I received a long–distance call from my Navy Headquarters, asking me to return to Tokyo.

> With the end of the war, my military career was over, since all Japanese forces were disbanded. I returned to my home village ... Though I was never accused, Gen. Douglas MacArthur summoned me to testify ... As I got off the train one day in Tokyo's Shibuya Station, I saw an American distributing literature.

> When I passed him, he handed me a pamphlet entitled "I Was a Prisoner of Japan"

(published by Bible Literature International) ... What I read was the fascinating episode which eventually changed my life ...

Fuchida continued:

Jake DeShazer ... volunteered for a secret mission with the Jimmy Doolittle Squadron – a surprise raid on Tokyo from the carrier *Hornet* ... After the bombing raid ... DeShazer found himself a prisoner of Japan ....

There in the Japanese P.O.W. camp, he read and read and eventually came to understand that the book was more than a historical classic ... The dynamic power of Christ which Jake DeShazer accepted into his life changed his entire attitude toward his captors. His hatred turned to love ...

Mitsuo Fuchida wrote further:

DeShazer ... returned to Japan as a missionary. And his story, printed in pamphlet form, was something I could not explain ... Since the American had found it in the Bible, I decided to purchase one myself, despite my traditionally Buddhist heritage ...

In the ensuing weeks, I read this book eagerly. I came to the climactic drama – the Crucifixion. I read in Luke 23:34 the prayer of Jesus Christ at His death: "Father, forgive them; for they know not what they do" ...

I was certainly one of those for whom He had prayed. The many men I had killed had been slaughtered in the name of patriotism, for I did not understand the love which Christ wishes to implant within every heart.

Right at that moment, I seemed to meet Jesus for the first time. I understood the meaning of His death as a substitute for my wickedness, and so in prayer, I requested Him to forgive my sins and change me from a bitter, disillusioned ex-pilot into a well-balanced Christian with purpose in living ...

I became a new person. My complete view on life was changed by the intervention of the Christ I had always hated and ignored before ...

Mitsuo Fuchida added:

I have traveled across Japan and the Orient introducing others to the One Who changed my life. I believe with all my heart that those who will direct Japan – and all other nations – in the decades to come must not ignore the message of Jesus Christ.

Youth must realize that He is the only hope for this troubled world ... I would give anything to retract my actions of twenty-nine years ago at Pearl Harbor, but it is impossible.

Mitsuo Fuchida concluded:

Instead, I now work at striking the death–blow to the basic hatred which infests the human heart and causes such tragedies. And that hatred cannot be uprooted without assistance from Jesus Christ.

CR

REV. MARTIN LUTHER KING, JR. "I HAVE A DREAM"

Martin Luther King, Jr. was born on January 15, 1929. He attended Booker T. Washington High School in Atlanta, 1942–44.

In 1944, Martin Luther King, Jr., attended Morehouse College in Atlanta, a college founded after the Civil War by Baptist minister Rev. William Jefferson White. Originally named Atlanta Baptist College, it was renamed after Henry Lyman Morehouse, secretary of the American Baptist Home Mission Society.

At Morehouse, King was a member of the debate team, student council, glee club, sociology club, and minister's union. In 1948, King, Jr., became a student at Crozer Theological Seminary in Upland, Pennsylvania. While a student, he attended Calvary Baptist Church in Chester, Pennsylvania.

In 1951, he graduated with a Bachelor of Divinity degree. He was ordained a Baptist preacher like his brother, Rev. A.D. King, pastor of Mount Vernon First Baptist Church in Newnan, Georgia, and like his father, Rev. "Daddy" King – Martin Luther King, Sr., who was pastor of Ebenezer Baptist Church in Atlanta, Georgia.

In 1954, King became pastor of Dexter Avenue Baptist Church in Montgomery, Alabama. In 1960, he became co–pastor with his father of Ebenezer Baptist Church in Atlanta. King formed the Southern Christian Leadership Conference, after which he rose to national prominence.

In 1957, Rev. Martin Luther King attended the Billy Graham Crusade in New York City. Graham wrote in his autobiography:

> One night civil rights leader Dr. Martin Luther King, Jr., whom I was pleased to count a friend, gave an eloquent opening prayer at the service; he also came at my invitation to one of our Team retreats during the Crusade to help us understand the racial situation in America more fully.

Becoming friends, Billy Graham shared a conversation with Rev. King:

> His father, who was called Big Mike, called him Little Mike. He asked me to call him just plain Mike.

Rev. King credited Billy Graham with reducing racial tension, as Graham even canceled a 1965 tour of Europe to preach crusades in Alabama, allowing the Gospel to bring healing between the races. Billy Graham stated:

> Jesus was not a white man; He was not a black man. He came from that part of the world that touches Africa and Asia and Europe. Christianity is not a white man's religion, and don't let anybody ever tell you that it's white or black. Christ belongs to all people; He belongs to the whole world.

Billy Graham wrote:

> My study of the Bible, leading me eventually to the conclusion that not only was racial inequality wrong but Christians especially should demonstrate love toward all peoples.

Martin Luther King, Jr., wrote:

Had it not been for the ministry of my good friend Dr. Billy Graham, my work in the Civil Rights Movement would not have been as successful as it has been.

Rev. King, Jr., stated:

• I see Israel as one of the great outposts of democracy in the world ... as a marvelous example of what can be done ... how desert land can be transformed into an oasis of brotherhood and democracy.

• Peace for Israel means security and that security must be a reality.

• I solemnly pledge to do my utmost to uphold the fair name of the Jews.

On April 16, 1963, Rev. Martin Luther King, Jr., wrote:

As the Apostle Paul carried the gospel of Jesus Christ ... so am I compelled to carry the gospel ... One day the South will know that when these disinherited children of God sat down at lunch counters, they were standing up for what is best in the American dream and for the most sacred values in our Judeo–Christian heritage.

Rev. Martin Luther King, Jr., as well as South African Archbishop Desmond Tutu, were influenced by the German Confessing Church leader Dietrich Bonhoeffer, who resisted the anti–Christian totalitarianism of Hitler's National Socialist Workers' Party.

Bonhoeffer was himself influenced by the black preacher, Adam Clayton Powell Sr., pastor of Harlem's Abyssinian Baptist Church, once the largest Protestant church in America.

Rev. Martin Luther King, Jr., was also influenced by Henry David Thoreau, who wrote in his book, *In Civil Disobedience* (1849): "That government is best which governs least." King was also influenced by the non-violent methods of India's Mahatma Gandhi who resisted Britain's globalist centralized big government.

Rev. Dr. Martin Luther King, Jr., warned August 28, 1963:

> Now is the time to open the doors of opportunity to all of God's children ... In the process of gaining our rightful place we must not be guilty of wrongful deeds. Let us not seek to satisfy our thirst for freedom by drinking from the cup of bitterness and hatred.
>
> We must forever conduct our struggle on the high plane of dignity and discipline. We must not allow our creative protest to degenerate into physical violence ...
>
> New militancy which has engulfed the Negro community must not lead us to a distrust of all white people, for many of our white brothers, as evidenced by their presence here today, have come to realize that their destiny is tied up with our destiny and their freedom is inextricably bound to our freedom. We cannot walk alone.

On April 16, 1963, Rev. King wrote:

> I must make two honest confessions to you, my Christian and Jewish brothers ... I stand in the middle of two opposing forces in the Negro community. One is a force of complacency ... The other force is one of bitterness and hatred, and it comes perilously close to advocating violence. It is expressed in the various black nationalist groups that are springing up across the nation, the largest and best-known being Elijah Muhammad's Muslim movement ...

Nourished by the Negro's frustration over the continued existence of racial discrimination, this movement is made up of people who have lost faith in America, who have absolutely repudiated Christianity, and who have concluded that the white man is an incorrigible "devil" ...

King continued:

I have tried to stand between these two forces, saying that we need emulate neither the "do–nothingism" of the complacent nor the hatred of the black nationalist.

For there is the more excellent way of love and non-violent protest. I am grateful to God that, through the influence of the Negro church, the way of non-violence became an integral part of our struggle ...

If our white brothers dismiss ... those of us who employ nonviolent direct action ... millions of Negroes will, out of frustration and despair, seek solace and security in black nationalist ideologies – a development that would inevitably lead to a frightening racial nightmare.

In his address at Montgomery, Alabama, December 31, 1955, Rev. King declared:

If you will protest courageously, and yet with dignity and Christian love, when the history books are written in future generations, the historians will have to pause and say, "There lived a great people–a black people–who injected new meaning and dignity into the veins of civilization."

On August 28, 1963, on the occasion of the Civil Rights March on Washington,

Martin Luther King, Jr., declared:

Now is the time to open the doors of opportunity to all of God's children. Now is the time to lift our nation from the quicksands of racial injustice to the solid rock of brotherhood ...

I still have a dream. It is a dream deeply rooted in the American dream. I have a dream that one day this nation will rise up and live out the true meaning of its creed: "We hold these truths to be self–evident; that all men are created equal."

I have a dream that one day on the red hills of Georgia the sons of former slaves and the sons of former slaveowners will be able to sit down together at the table of brotherhood ... I have a dream that my four little children will one day live in a nation where they will not be judged by the color of their skin, but by the content of their character ...

I have a dream ... where little black boys and black girls will be able to join hands with little white boys and white girls and walk together as sisters and brothers. I have a dream today. I have a dream that one day every valley shall be exalted, every hill and mountain shall be made low, the rough places will be made plain, and the crooked places will be made straight, and the glory of the Lord shall be revealed, and all flesh shall see it together ...

With this faith we will be able to work together, to pray together, to struggle together, to go to jail together, to stand up for freedom together, knowing that we will be free one day. This will be the day when all of God's children will be able to sing with new meaning, "My country 'tis of thee, sweet land of liberty, of thee I sing. Land where my fathers died, land of the Pilgrims' pride, from every mountainside, let freedom ring ...

When we let freedom ring, when we let it ring from every village and every hamlet, from every state and every city, we will be able to speed up that day when all of God's children, black men and white men, Jews and Gentiles, Protestants and Catholics, will be able to join hands and sing in the words of the old Negro spiritual, "Free at last! Free at last! Thank God Almighty, we are free at last!"

Rev. Martin Luther King, Jr., was assassinated April 4, 1968. On November 2, 1983, Republican President Ronald Reagan signed the bill to make Rev. Martin Luther King, Jr.'s birthday a National Holiday, observed the 3rd Monday in January, stating:

Dr. King had awakened something strong and true, a sense that true justice must be colorblind, and that among white and black Americans, as he put it, "Their destiny is tied up with our destiny, and their freedom is inextricably bound to our freedom; we cannot walk alone."

On March 6, 1984, President Ronald Reagan mentioned Rev. King in his remarks at the annual convention of the National Association of Evangelicals, meeting at the Hyatt Regency Hotel in Columbus, Ohio:

During the civil rights struggles of the fifties and early sixties, millions worked for equality in the name of their Creator. Civil rights leaders like Dr. Martin Luther King based all their efforts on the claim that black or white, each of us is a child of God. And they stirred our nation to the very depths of its soul.

President George H.W. Bush proclaimed 1990 the International Year of Bible Reading, stating:

> The historic speeches of Abraham Lincoln and Dr. Martin Luther King, Jr., provide compelling evidence of the role Scripture played in shaping the struggle against slavery and discrimination.

On January 20, 1997, Rev. Billy Graham delivered the invocation just prior to the Second Inauguration of President Bill Clinton, stating:

> Oh, Lord, help us to be reconciled first to you and secondly to each other. May Dr. Martin Luther King's dream finally come true for all of us. Help us to learn our courtesy to our fellow countrymen, that comes from the one who taught us that "whatever you want me to do to you, do also to them."

On February 16, 2002, Dr. James Dobson addressed 3,500 attendees at the National Religious Broadcaster's convention:

> Those of you who do feel that the church has no responsibility in the cultural area ... Suppose it were ... 1963, and Martin Luther King is sitting in a Birmingham jail and he is released. And he goes to a church, yes, a church. And from that church, he comes out into the streets of Birmingham and marches for civil rights. Do you oppose that? Is that a violation of the separation of church and state?

Martin Luther King, Jr.'s niece, Dr. Alveda King, told *The Call Detroit,* November 11, 2011:

> My father, Rev. A.D. King, is brother to Martin ... Uncle M.L., Daddy, and their earthly father, Daddy King were preachers of the Gospel of Jesus Christ ...
>
> Daddy King rescued me from abortion in 1950. You can read the story in my book: HOW CAN THE DREAM SURVIVE IF WE MURDER THE CHILDREN? ... When my mother wanted to abort me, Daddy King told her: "No. They are lying to you. She is not a lump of flesh. She is a little girl, with bright skin and bright red hair. She will be a blessing to many."

So you see, this little girl who is part Irish, part African and part Native American is standing before you today to bear witness of Acts 17:26, that of One Blood, God made all people to live on earth in a Beloved Community, and one day, to live in Eternity with Him. So we are one human race, not separate races.

⊗

BILLY GRAHAM "IF EVER WE NEEDED GOD'S HELP, IT IS NOW"

"America has gone a long way down the wrong road. We must turn around and go back and change roads. If ever we needed God's help, it is now"–stated Billy Graham, as he received the Congressional Gold Medal, May 2, 1996.

Born November 7, 1918, he wanted to be a baseball player, but after attending a revival at age 16, his life changed. He was born again, followed a call to the ministry, and eventually became an internationally renown evangelist, preaching to millions around the world.

Billy Graham had an unprecedented friendship with world leaders and every U.S. President, from President Truman to President Trump. President Eisenhower stated March 21, 1956:

This is what I see in Billy Graham – A man who clearly understands that any advance in the world has got to be accompanied by a clear realization that man is, after all, a spiritual being.

John F. Kennedy told the Presidential Prayer Breakfast, March 1, 1962:

We bear great responsibilities and great burdens not only to ourselves in this country but to so many around the world ... I commend ... Reverend Billy Graham, who has served this cause about which I speak so well here and around the world. He has, I think, transmitted this most important quality of our common commitments to faith in a way which makes all of us particularly proud.

Ronald Reagan introduced Billy Graham at a California rally, stating:

> Why is a representative of government here? To welcome with humble pride a man whose mission in life has been to remind us that in all our seeking ... the answer to each problem is to be found in the simple words of Jesus of Nazareth, who urged us to love one another.

Billy Graham stated:

> In a world that might say one vote doesn't matter ... it does matter because each person is of infinite worth and value to God ... Your vote is a declaration of importance as a person and a citizen.

He added: "Bad politicians are elected by good people who don't vote." In answering a question about voting, Billy Graham stated on July 28, 2016:

> The Bible says we should do everything we possibly can to be good citizens and work for the betterment of our society, and one of the ways we can do this is by voting. God tells us to "seek the peace and prosperity of the city to which I have carried you" (Jeremiah 29:7).
>
> Rightly or wrongly, you say you're disillusioned by what you see in politics today. But how will it be changed? Let me tell you how it won't be changed: It won't be changed if concerned people refuse to vote! It also won't be changed if good people refuse to run for office, or if no one votes for them. In other words, staying away from the voting booth may only perpetuate the problems you see.
>
> Although this election has passed, don't let another one go by without your intelligent

involvement. Christians in the first century didn't have the privilege of voting; Caesar was a dictator, not elected by popular vote. But those early believers were commanded to do the one thing they could do to make the world a better place:

They were told to pray. The Apostle Paul wrote, "I urge, then, first of all, that petitions, prayers, intercession and thanksgiving be made for all people—for kings and all those in authority" (1 Timothy 2:1–2). Our world will never be perfect—not until Christ returns. But in the meantime, God wants to use us to overcome sin and establish a more just world for His glory.

Upon receiving the Congressional Gold Medal, May 2, 1996, Billy Graham gave a message, "The Hope for America":

After World War II ... we had the opportunity to rule the world ... Something has happened since those days and there is much about America that is no longer good ... the list is almost endless ... We have confused liberty with license – and we are paying the awful price. We are a society poised on the brink of self–destruction ...

What is the problem? The real problem is within ourselves ... I believe the fundamental crisis of our time is a crisis of the spirit. We have lost sight of the moral and spiritual principles on which this nation was established – principles drawn largely from the Judeo–Christian tradition as found in the Bible ... What must be done? Let me briefly suggest three things.

FIRST, we must repent. In the depths of the American Civil War, Abraham Lincoln called for special days of public repentance and prayer. Our need for repentance is no less today ... What does repentance mean? Repentance means to change our thinking and our way of living. It means to turn from our sins and to commit ourselves to God and His will.

Over 2700 years ago the Old Testament prophet Isaiah declared "Seek the Lord while he may be found, call on Him while He is near. Let the wicked forsake his way, and the evil man his thoughts. Let him turn to the Lord, and He will have mercy on him, and to our God, for He will freely pardon" (Isaiah 55: 6–7, NIV) ...

Billy Graham continued:

SECOND, we must commit our lives to God, and to the moral and spiritual truths that have made this nation great. Think how different our nation would be if we sought to follow the simple and yet profound injunctions of the Ten Commandments and the Sermon on the Mount. But we must respond to God, Who is offering us forgiveness, mercy, supernatural help, and the power to change ...

THIRD, our commitment must be translated into action – in our homes, in our neighborhoods, and in our society. Jesus taught there are only two roads in life. One is the broad road that is easy and well–traveled, but which leads to destruction.

The other, He said, is the narrow road of truth and faith that at times is hard and lonely, but which leads to life and salvation ... What are YOU going to do? ... As I look out across this distinguished group gathered here, I see more than a few men and women who have what it takes, under God, to lead our country forward "through the night."

Rev. Billy Graham warned October 27, 2015:

Suppose persecution were to come to the church in America, as it has come in other countries. The immunity to persecution that Christians in our country have experienced in the past two or three centuries is unusual. Christ strongly warned Christians that to follow Him would not be popular, and that in most circumstances it would mean cross–bearing and persecution.

The Bible says that all who "desire to live godly in Christ Jesus will suffer persecution" (2 Timothy 3:12). Jesus said that as the time of His return draws nigh, "They will seize you and persecute you" (Luke 21:12). We have no scriptural foundation for believing that we can forever escape being persecuted for Christ's sake. The normal condition for Christians is that we should suffer persecution.

He continued:

Are you willing to face persecution and death for Christ's sake? Since we have experienced little religious persecution in this country, it is likely that under pressure many would deny Christ. Those who shout the loudest about their faith may surrender soonest. Many who boast of being courageous would be cowardly. Many who say, "Though all others deny Christ, yet I will never deny Him," would be the first to warm their hands at the campfires of the enemy.

Jesus, in speaking of the last times, warned, "Then they will hand you over to be persecuted and kill you, and you will be hated by all nations for My name's sake" (Matthew 24:9). The Scripture says, "because iniquity will abound, the love of many will grow cold" (Matthew 24:12). The apostle Paul, referring to the coming evil day, said, "Therefore take up the whole armor of God that you may be able to resist in the evil day, and having done all, to stand" (Ephesians 6:13) ...

Even though most Americans see the storm clouds gathering on the horizon, by and large we are making few preparations to meet God. This is a time for repentance and faith. It is a time for soul–searching, to see if our anchor holds.

Have you been to the cross where Christ shed His blood for your sins? Have you had the past forgiven? Have you come by faith, confessing that you are a sinner and receiving Christ as your Savior? I tell you that this cross is the only place of refuge in the midst of the storm of judgment that is fast approaching. Make sure of your relationship with God ...

He concluded:

We must fortify ourselves by meditating upon the person of Christ ... Christ must be vitally real to us if we are to prove loyal to Him in the hours of crisis. Today our nation ranks as the greatest power on the face of the earth. But if we put our trust in armed might instead of Almighty God, the coming conflict could conceivably go against us. History and the Bible indicate that mechanical and material might are insufficient in times of great crisis.

We need the inner strength that comes from a personal, vital relationship with God's Son, Jesus Christ. The wheels of God's judgment can be heard by discerning souls across the length and breadth of nations. Things are happening fast! The need for a return to God has never been more urgent. The words of Isaiah are appropriate for us today: "Seek the Lord while He may be found ... and He will have mercy upon him, and to our God, for He will abundantly pardon."

On November 7, 2017, Franklin Graham sent via Twitter a photo of his father: "My father *@BillyGraham* turns 99 years old today. That means he's entering his 100th year – it has been an amazing journey." President Donald Trump tweeted back: "Franklin, such a great photo. HAPPY 99th BIRTHDAY to your father *@BillyGraham! twitter.com/franklin_graham*"

When Billy Graham died, February 21, 2018, President Donald Trump ordered:

As a mark of respect for the memory of Reverend Billy Graham, I hereby order ... that on the day of his interment, the flag of the United States shall be flown at half–staff at the White House and upon all public buildings.

Speaking of his own death, Graham once said:

Someday you will read or hear that Billy Graham is dead. Don't you believe a word of it. I shall be more alive than I am now. I will just have changed my address. I will have gone into the presence of God.

As he received the Congressional Gold Medal, May 2, 1996, Billy Graham exhorted:

If ever we needed spiritual renewal, it is now. And it can begin today in each one of our lives, as we repent before God and yield ourselves to Him and His Word.

CR

NASA & ASTRONAUTS' PRAYER ON THE MOON – "WHEN I CONSIDER THE HEAVENS, THE WORK OF THY FINGERS, THE MOON & THE STARS WHICH THOU HAS ORDAINED..."

"One small step for a man, one giant leap for mankind," stated Astronaut Neil Armstrong, July 20, 1969, as he became the first man to walk on the moon, almost 238,900 miles away from the Earth. The second man on the moon was Colonel Buzz Aldrin, who described it as "magnificent desolation."

Aldrin earned a Ph.D. from M.I.T. and helped develop the technology necessary for the mission, especially the complicated lunar module rendezvous with the command module. Buzz Aldrin's popularity was the inspiration for the character "Buzz Lightyear" in Pixar's animated movie *Toy Story* (1995).

He shared a story, "An Astronaut Tells of a little-known but Significant Event on the Moon" (*Guideposts Magazine,* October 1970; *Return to Earth,* Random House, 1973). Before the two astronauts stepped out of the Lunar Module onto the moon's surface, there was a planned time of rest. Buzz Aldrin asked for radio silence because NASA was fighting a lawsuit brought by atheist Madalyn Murray O'Hair. She objected to the previous Apollo 8 crew reading the first chapter of the Book of Genesis in their Christmas 1968 radio transmission.

During the radio silence, Buzz Aldrin then privately partook of communion, stating:

For several weeks prior to the scheduled lift-off of Apollo 11 back in July, 1969, the pastor of our church, Dean Woodruff, and I had been struggling to find the right symbol for the first lunar landing. We wanted to express our feeling that what man was doing in this mission transcended electronics and computers and rockets ...

Dean often speaks at our church, Webster Presbyterian, just outside of Houston, about the many meanings of the communion service. "One of the principal symbols," Dean says, "is that God reveals Himself in the common elements of everyday life." Traditionally, these elements are bread and wine–common foods in Bible days and typical products of man's labor.

One day while I was at Cape Kennedy working with the sophisticated tools of the space effort, it occurred to me that these tools were the typical elements of life today. I wondered if it might be possible to take communion on the moon, symbolizing the thought that God was revealing Himself there too, as man reached out into the universe. For there are many of us in the NASA program who do trust that what we are doing is part of God's eternal plan for man.

Webster Presbyterian is known as the Church of the Astronauts as John Glenn, Buzz Aldrin, Jerry Carr, Charlie Bassett, and Roger Chaffee were members during their time at NASA. Another church member, Jack Kinzler, built the flag left on the moon. Aldrin continued:

I spoke with Dean about the idea as soon as I returned home, and he was enthusiastic. "I could carry the bread in a plastic packet, the way regular inflight food is wrapped. And the wine also–there will be just enough gravity on the moon for liquid to pour. I'll be able to drink normally from a cup. Dean, I wonder if you could look around for a little chalice that I could take with me ... coming from the church?" The next week Dean showed me a graceful silver cup. I hefted it and was pleased to find that it was light enough to take along. Each astronaut is allowed a few personal items on a flight; the wine chalice would be in my personal–preference kit.

Dean made special plans for two special communion services at Webster Presbyterian Church. One would be held just prior to my leaving Houston for Cape Kennedy, when I would join the other members in a dedication service. The second would take place two weeks later, Sunday, July 20, when Neil Armstrong and I were scheduled to be on the surface of the moon. On that Sunday the church back home would gather for communion, while I joined them as close as possible to the same hour, taking communion inside the lunar module, all of us meaning to represent in this small way not only our local church but the Church as a whole.

The *Houston Chronicle* and the *Huffington Post* have published articles about Buzz Aldrin's communion on the moon. Aldrin continued:

We decided we would say nothing about the communion service until after the moonshot ... I had a question about which scriptural passage to use ... and came up at last with John 15:5. It seemed to fit perfectly. I wrote the passage on a slip of paper to be carried aboard *Eagle* along with the communion elements. Dean would read the same passage at the full congregation service held back home that same day.

Buzz Aldrin wrote further:

Saturday, just prior to the ... communion services ... the flight physician arrived and set up elaborate precautions against crew contamination ... We had to wear sterile masks and talk to the reporters from within a special partition. The doctor was taking no chances. A cold germ, a flu virus, and the whole shot might have to be aborted. I felt I had to tell him about the big church service scheduled for the next morning. When I did, he wasn't at all happy ... "What about a private service?" ... I called the doctor about the smaller service and he agreed ...

Aldrin added:

So the next day, Sunday, shortly after the end of the 11 o'clock service, my wife, Joan, and our oldest boy, Mike ... went to the church. There we met Dean, his wife, Floy, and our close family friend Tom Manison, elder of the church, and his wife. The seven of us went in to the now–empty sanctuary. On the communion table were two loaves of bread, one for now, the other for two weeks from now.

Beside the two loaves were two chalices, one of them the small cup the church was giving me for the service on the moon. We took communion. At the end of the service Dean tore off a corner of the second loaf of bread and handed it to me along with the tiny chalice. Within a few hours I was on my way to Cape Kennedy. What happened there, of course, the whole world knows.

The Saturn 5 rocket gave us a rough ride at first, but the rest of the trip was smooth. On the day of the moon landing, we awoke at 5:30 a.m., Houston time. Neil and

I separated from Mike Collins in the command module. Our powered descent was right on schedule, and perfect except for one unforeseeable difficulty. The automatic guidance system would have taken *Eagle* to an area with huge boulders. Neil had to steer the *Eagle* to a more suitable terrain. With only seconds worth of fuel left, we touched down at 3:30 p.m.

Mission Control was nervous, as the *Eagle* was descending too fast. The on-board guidance system computer sounded an alarm — a switch was on, causing the radar to look both down at the moon's surface and up at the *Columbia,* in case the landing had to be aborted. The computer was dithering between the upward and downward signals.

Armstrong switched to manually land the craft, with Aldrin relaying instrument readings, as propulsion rockets kicked up a cloud of moon dust, obscuring vision of the boulders below. Upon landing, Neil Armstrong radioed: "Houston, Tranquility Base here. The *Eagle* has landed." Mission Control's CAPCOM (Capsule Communicator), Charles Duke, who was later on Apollo 16, replied: "Roger, Twank ... Tranquility, we copy you on the ground. You got a bunch of guys about to turn blue. We're breathing again. Thanks a lot!"

Aldrin later wrote: "Now Neil and I were sitting inside *Eagle,* while Mike circled in lunar orbit unseen in the black sky above us."

Mike Collins took the photo of the *Eagle* separating from the command module *Columbia,* and drifting down toward the moon. He was now alone, crossing to the dark side of the moon, out of radio contact with Earth, nearly a quarter of a million miles away. He was the second most distant *solo* human traveler after Astronaut John Young of Apollo

10's dress rehearsal moon landing.

Mike Collins orbited the moon 30 times, at an altitude of 57 miles. He wrote:

> This venture has been structured for three men, and I consider my third to be as necessary as either of the other two. I don't mean to deny a feeling of solitude. It is there, reinforced by the fact that radio contact with the Earth abruptly cuts off the instant I disappear behind the moon. I am alone now, truly alone, and absolutely isolated from any known life. I am it.
>
> If a count were taken, the score would be three billion plus two over on the other side of the moon, and one plus God knows what on this side.

The Guardian, July 18, 2009, printed Collins' comments, that "not since Adam has any human known such solitude ... with no one to talk to except his tape recorder," and that he was "sweating like a nervous bride" until the *Eagle* returned:

> Collins' deepest fear: that he would be the only survivor of an Apollo 11 disaster ... Despite their apparent calm ... no one was more stressed than Collins ... (He) was obsessed with the reliability of the ascent engine of Armstrong and Aldrin's lander, *Eagle.* It had never been fired on the moon's surface before ... Should the engine fail to ignite, Armstrong and Aldrin would be stranded on the moon — where they would die when their oxygen ran out. Or if it failed to burn for at least seven minutes, then the two astronauts would either crash back on to the moon or be stranded in low orbit around it, beyond the reach of Collins in his mothership, *Columbia.*

On the moon's surface, Buzz Aldrin recounted:

In a little while after our scheduled meal period, Neil would give the signal to step down the ladder onto the powdery surface of the moon. Now was the moment for communion. So I unstowed the elements in their flight packets. I put them and the scripture reading on the little table in front of the abort guidance system computer ...

Then I called back to Houston. "Houston, this is *Eagle*. This is the LM Pilot speaking. I would like to request a few moments of silence. I would like to invite each person listening in, wherever and whomever he may be, to contemplate for a moment the events of the past few hours and to give thanks in his own individual way" ...

On World Communion Sunday ... many Christians through the world will unite in spirit as they—each in his own church, according to his own tradition—participate in celebrating the Lord's Supper ... For me, this meant taking communion. In the radio blackout I opened the little plastic packages which contained bread and wine. I poured the wine into the chalice our church had given me. In the one-sixth gravity of the moon the wine curled slowly and gracefully up the side of the cup.

It was interesting to think that the very first liquid ever poured on the moon, and the first food eaten there, were communion elements. And so, just before I partook of the elements, I read the words, which I had chosen to indicate our trust that as man probes into space we are in fact acting in Christ ... I sensed especially strongly my unity with our church back home, and with the Church everywhere.

I read: "I am the vine, you are the branches. Whoever remains in me, and I in
him, will bear much fruit; for you can do nothing without me."

Webster Presbyterian Church keeps the chalice used on the moon and commemorates
the event each year on the Sunday closest to July 20.

Armstrong and Aldrin spent a total of 21 hours and 37 minutes on the moon's surface.
Armstrong took the historic photo of Buzz Aldrin saluting the American Flag. After their
moon walk, they climbed back into the *Eagle*. Their large spacesuits, which included life
support backpacks, made maneuvering difficult and the circuit breaker, which controlled
ignition for the lift-off rockets, was accidentaly broken. This potentially serious accident
was fixed with the help of a felt-tipped pen.

A little known event in the USA–USSR Space Race was that the Soviet's launched
an unmanned lunar landing module, *Luna 15*, at the same time, and attempted to land it
as close as possible to the *Eagle* landing site. Just two hours before Armstrong and Aldrin
blasted off from the moon, Russia's *Luna 15* crashed landed in the nearby Mare Crisium.

To reduce weight, Armstrong and Aldrin threw out unnecessary moon walk equipment,
then re-compressed the *Eagle*. The *Eagle* lifted off and successfully re-docked with the
Columbia. As they were returning to Earth, July 23, 1969, Buzz Aldrin stated via television:

This has been far more than three men on a mission to the moon ... Personally,
in reflecting on the events of the past several days, a verse from Psalms comes to
mind. "When I consider the heavens, the work of Thy fingers, the moon and the
stars, which Thou hast ordained; What is man that Thou art mindful of him?"

Neil Armstrong added:

> To all the other people that are listening and watching tonight, God bless you. Good night from Apollo 11.

Armstrong later addressed a joint session of Congress, September 16, 1969:

> To those of you who have advocated looking high we owe our sincere gratitude, for you have granted us the opportunity to see some of the grandest views of the Creator.

This echoed an earlier comment by Apollo 8 Astronaut Frank Borman, who, when told a Russian cosmonaut did not see God in space, replied: "I didn't see Him, but I saw His evidence."

In November of 1969, Apollo 12 Astronauts Pete Conrad and Alan Bean spent over 31 hours on the moon. Bean later became a painter of dramatic moonscapes, one of which was titled *We Came In Peace For All Mankind,* depicting Astronaut Jim Irwin kneeling on the moon with hands folded in prayer.

In 1970, Apollo 13 had an oxygen tank explode, damaging the spacecraft. President Nixon called the nation to join in prayer for the Astronauts' safe return.

In February of 1971, Apollo 14 Astronaut Edgar Mitchell left a microfilm copy of the King James Bible on the moon inside lunar module *Antares.* Beginning July 30, 1971, Apollo 15 Astronauts James Irwin and David Scott spent almost 3 days on the moon. Irwin wrote:

> Being on the moon had a profound spiritual impact upon my life. Before I entered space with the Apollo 15 mission in July of 1971, I was ... a silent Christian, but I feel the Lord sent me to the moon so I could return to the earth and share his Son, Jesus Christ.

Irwin later became an evangelical minister, proclaiming: "Jesus walking on the earth is more important than man walking on the moon."

In 1972, Astronauts Charles Duke and John Young flew to the moon on Apollo 16, exploring the moon's rugged Descartes region. Duke later spoke at a Prayer Rally during the Texas State's Republican Convention in San Antonio's Lila Cockrell Theatre, June 22, 1996:

> I have been before kings and prime ministers, junta leaders and dictators, businessmen and beggars, rich and poor, black and white ... One of the most touching times was in the office of one of the cabinet ministers in Israel ... After the introduction I was asked to share my walk on the moon with the Israeli minister.
>
> "Mr. Minister," I began, "I was able to look back at the earth from the moon and hold up my hand and underneath this hand was the earth. The thought occurred to me that underneath my hand were four billion people. I couldn't see Europe, America, the Middle East. I couldn't see blacks or whites, Jews or Orientals, just spaceship earth. I realized we needed to learn to love one another, and I believed that with that love and our technical expertise, we could solve all of mankind's problems ..."

He added:

> The promises of the Bible are true and, I believe, speak the truth in every area — whether it be in spiritual matters, nutrition, history, or even science ... In 1972 aboard Apollo 16, I saw with my own eyes what is written in the Scriptures.
>
> In Isaiah 40:22 it says "It is He that sitteth upon the circle of the earth." And in Job 26:7, it is written "He hangeth the earth upon nothing." Who told Isaiah that

the earth was a circle? ... And how did the writer of Job know that the earth hung upon nothing? ... This is the Lord I love and serve. This is the Lord who transformed my life. This is the Lord who transformed my marriage.

I used to say I could live ten thousand years and never have an experience as thrilling as walking on the moon. But the excitement and satisfaction of that walk doesn't begin to compare with my walk with Jesus, a walk that lasts forever. I thought Apollo 16 would be my crowning glory, but the crown that Jesus gives will not tarnish or fade away. His crown will last throughout all eternity ...

Charles Duke concluded:

Not everyone has the opportunity to walk on the moon, but everybody has the opportunity to walk with the Son. It costs billions of dollars to send someone to the moon, but walking with Jesus is free, the Gift of God. "For by Grace are ye saved through faith, and that not of yourselves, it is the gift of God, not of works, lest any man should boast."

You don't need to go to the moon to find God. I didn't find God in space – I found him in the front seat of my car on Highway 46 in New Braunfels, Texas, when I opened my heart to Jesus. And my life hasn't been the same since. Now I can truly look up at the moon and the stars and with the prophets of old exclaim, "The heavens declare the glory of God, and the firmament showeth His handiwork."

❧
DR. D. JAMES KENNEDY
"BRINGING THE GOSPEL TO AMERICA & TO THE WORLD"

Dr. D. James Kennedy was one of the most listened to Christian ministers in America, presenting the Gospel in his rational and forthright way via television, radio and the internet. His virtuous life and dignified, loving style of preaching has helped equip others to share the Gospel of Salvation around the world.

Dr. Kennedy who entered the presence of his Savior, Jesus Christ on September 5, 2007, began his Christian life in 1953 after he was startled awake one Sunday morning by a preacher's stern question coming out of his clock radio. "Suppose you were to die today and stand before God" the voice boomed, "And He were to ask you 'What right do you have to enter into my Heaven?' – what would you say?"

Dr. Kennedy soon discovered the answer, was converted to Christ, and shortly thereafter was called into the Gospel ministry. He served for 48 years as Senior Minister of Coral Ridge Presbyterian Church in Ft. Lauderdale, Florida. A modest mission church of 45 people when he arrived in 1959, the rocketing growth of the church made it, for 15 years the fastest growing Presbyterian church in America, with his messages being broadcast into millions of homes nationwide.

Decision Magazine named the church "One of the five great churches of North America." Dr. Kennedy founded Westminster Academy in 1971 a Pre–K to 12th grade Christian Academy, and Knox Theological Seminary in 1989. The Lead Pastor of Coral Ridge Presbyterian Church is Rob Pacienza, a graduate of both Westminster and Knox, with a Master of Divinity.

In 2005, Dr. Kennedy was inducted into the National Religious Broadcasters Hall of Fame. In 1999, he was honored on the floor of the United States Congress.

Dr. Kennedy developed the lay witnessing program Evangelism Explosion, which has spread to every nation and territory. Under the leadership of President Dr. John Sorensen, EE has sparked explosive church growth around the world. One of the EE missionaries, Gary Letchworth, has personally shared the Gospel in every country in Asia, and helped arrange for the training of an EE leader in virtually every nation. Over 200,000 nationals in all those countries from Japan to Turkey were trained to share their faith in Christ, and they are now leading 2 million to Christ in Asia every year. Worldwide now, about 10 million are being led to Christ each year through EE.

D. James Kennedy Ministries began a media outreach in 1974 as Coral Ridge Ministries with the mission of bringing the Gospel to America and the world. It included a weekly half-hour radio program *Truths That Transform;* weekly television program *The Coral Ridge Hour* (now *Truths That Transform*); the website www.DJamesKennedy.org; the monthly *Impact* newsletter; and other print and video resources.

DJKM continues impacting the world under the direction of its President Dr. Frank

Wright, a leader who has experience as the founding director of the Center for Christian Statesmanship in Washington, DC; President and CEO of the National Religious Broadcasters; and acting as the President and COO of Salem Communication Corporation.

Overseeing the television programs *Truths that Transforms* and *Kennedy Classics* is Director of Creative Productions John Rabe. Senior Producer and an on-air host at DJKM is Dr. Jerry Newcombe.

Dr. Newcombe co-authored 17 of Dr. Kennedy's 65 books, such as: *What If Jesus Had Never Been Born?*; *What If The Bible Had Never Been Written?*; *What If America Were A Christian Nation Again"*; *Who Is This Jesus: Is He Risen?'* and *Christ's Passion: The Power and the Promise.*

Many of Dr. Kennedy's profound statements are recorded in Dr. Jerry Newcombe's book, *The Wit & Wisdom of D. James Kennedy* (2013):

• The greatest ability that the Christian needs is availability. Are you available to God? Are you available to Him today and each day to use you?

• This is a nation that was born of the Bible, even as *Newsweek* said some years ago, that historians are now coming to realize, that it was the Bible, even more than the Constitution, that founded the nation of America.

• The Pilgrims were willing to cross this wild and ferocious desert of the ocean and go into the midst of savages all because of the Word of God, which was such a precious treasure. Many of us have two, three, four, or five Bibles in our homes, and yet we spend little time really searching them, reading them, or have them in our heart.

• It is not until we have embraced Jesus Christ, the Conquerer of the grave, that One could say "Because I live ye shall live also" (John 14:19) and "whosoever liveth and believeth in me shall never truly die" (John 11;26) that we can stand up and say "Give me liberty or give me death." It was the same Patrick Henry who said "There is a book worth more than all other books ever printed – the Scriptures."

• And yet, my friend, take heart. God did not make you to be a loser. He created you to be a winner, and that is what He is able to make you into. Christ is the Conquerer of the dead and of the angels of darkness and of Satan himself. He can well lead us in "triumph" if we yield ourselves to Him.

ೞ

PHYLLIS SCHLAFLY

Phyllis Schlafly was a national leader of the conservative movement since the publication of her best-selling 1964 book *A Choice Not an Echo.* She created the pro-family movement in 1972 when she started her national volunteer organization called Eagle Forum.

In a ten year battle, Mrs. Schlafly led the pro-family movement to victory over the principal legislative goal of the feminists, called the Equal Rights Amendment. An articulate, successful opponent of the radical feminist movement, she debated on college campuses more frequently than any other conservative.

She was named one of the hundred most influential women of the 21st century by *Ladies Home Journal.* Mrs. Schlafly's monthly newsletter called *The Phyllis Schlafly Report* was published for 50 years. Her syndicated column appeared in 100 newspapers and on many conservative websites.

She was the author or editor of 27 books on subjects from the family to feminism including: *The Power of the Positive Woman; Feminist Fantasies; The Supremacists–The Tyranny of Judges and How to Stop It; No Higher Power–Obama's War on Religious Freedom; Strike from Space* on nuclear strategy; *Child Abuse in the Classroom; Who Will Rock the Cradle;* and to teach phonics, *First Reader;* and *Turbo Reader.*

Phyllis Schlafly's 3-minute-a-day, 5-days-a-week radio commentaries ran from 1983 for over 3 decades, and were heard daily by millions of listeners on 600 stations. Her weekly radio talk show on education, called Eagle Forum Live, ran from 1989 to 2016 on Saturdays on over 100 stations. She also did weekly television commentaries on *CBS Morning News* (1974–1975) and *CNN* (1980–1983). She has appeared on almost every network news and public affairs program.

Mrs. Schlafly was a lawyer and testified before more than 50 Congressional and State Legislative committees on the Constitution, national defense and family issues. Phyllis was named the 1992 Illinois Mother of the Year. She and her late husband of 44 years raised their six children and taught them all to read before they entered school. All of them had outstanding academic success including three lawyers, one physician, one Ph.D. Mathematician, and a successful businesswoman.

On a personal note, as the author of this book, my husband's mother worked with Phyllis on pro-life and pro-family events. We watched Phyllis work diligently into her 80's to protect and preserve traditional family values that are the basis of American society. If only we could all give so much of our lives to preserve pro-life and pro-family values! Her dedication, diligence and courage remain an example to all of us to stand up and articulate our values in a changing society.

Phyllis Schlafly wrote:

• It is long overdue for parents to realize they have the right and duty to protect our children against the intolerant evolutionists.

• The most dangerous area where our laws are not being faithfully executed are the laws designed to protect Americans against the millions of aliens who enter our country illegally every year.

• A country is not sovereign if we cannot control who comes in.

• How can we protect homeland security unless the government stops the invasion of illegal aliens.

• What you can learn from life is, first of all, that anybody can be a leader. I developed it, I worked at it. Also, that the grassroots can organize and take on all the powers that be and defeat them. That is the lesson.

• Remember, those that wait upon the Lord will rise up with wings like Eagles, and they will run and not be weary ... The battle goes on year after year, and we need all of you young people to join us in battle.

CR

THE 45TH PRESIDENT: "GOD'S LOVE REDEEMS THE WORLD – WE ARE PROTECTING THE SANCTITY OF LIFE & THE FAMILY AS THE FOUNDATION OF OUR SOCIETY"

In 2015, many Americans were very concerned about the future of their country. Under the previous President, billions of American taxpayer dollars were given to enemies in Iran, the economy was struggling, businesses were moving overseas, healthcare costs tripled, jobs became scarce, and student loan interest was multiplying to a point that young people could not afford to do anything but pay down their college loans.

Police were being attacked and riots were burning down cities. Thoughts of socialism became appealing to some desperate citizens, with most not knowing where that would lead.

Then in June of 2015, a brave millionaire stood up and declared that "We will make America strong again. We will make America proud again. We will make America safe again. We will make America great again." This resonated in the hearts and prayers of citizens suffering all over the country.

Trump was the very definition of the American success story. He had always dreamed big and pushed the boundaries of what is possible. He devoted his life to building businesses, jobs, and the American dream, like many of the financially successful founding fathers who risked their "lives ... fortunes, and ... sacred honor," for future generations of Americans.

The President's wife, Melania, is herself a success story. A Slovene–born American who speaks five languages, she is the only First Lady who is a naturalized citizen. In her role as First Lady, the beautiful Mrs. Trump focuses her time on the many issues that affect children in her "BE BEST" campaign. She spends much of her time compassionately meeting with children who are patients in hospitals and care centers, and visiting schools. She is raising awareness of the dangers of opioid abuse and is focused on the total well-being of children.

Donald Trump was elected in November 2016 in the largest electoral college landslide for a Republican in 28 years. Since then, he has worked hard to follow through on his promises, without even accepting a salary, which he donates to benefit veterans. He jump–started America's economy into record growth, increased jobs and worker take–home pay, and helped the unemployment rates for blacks to reach a record low. As of May 2019, wages grew faster than 3% for 10 months in a row. The Department of Labor announced $1.5 million in grants to recruit, train and retain more women in quality careers.

He has promoted fair and reciprocal trade which includes exiting TPP, renegotiating NAFTA, and securing major bilateral deals with trade partners. He removed much of the red tape the previous administration implemented, thus ending unnecessary regulations that stifled economic growth. He reversed years of policies that kept America from energy independence, resulting in America becoming the world's top oil producer. He partnered with local law enforcement agencies in an effort to bring security back to our cities.

When ancient Israel returned from captivity, the man God chose was neither a politician nor a priest, but a builder whose name was Nehemiah. The first step in rebuilding the nation was to build a wall around Jerusalem to protect its citizens from enemy attack. President Trump has worked to build a wall to enforce immigration laws and to prevent a humanitarian crisis.

Millions of helpless immigrants have flooded into cities like Los Angeles, and states along the border, encouraged by Democrats in Congress who want to increase an entitlement–dependent voter base. Thanks to pressure from the Trump administration, Mexico is increasing its border security, deploying thousands of its own national guard troops.

The President is working to protect the most helpless among us – the unborn. On January 20, 2018, he followed the example of President Ronald Reagan by addressing the thousands who gathered for the annual March for Life:

> The March for Life is a movement born out of love ... You love every child, born and unborn, because you believe that every life is sacred, that every child is a precious gift from God. We know that life is the greatest miracle of all. We see it in the eyes of every new mother who cradles that wonderful, innocent, and glorious newborn child in her loving arms ... Because of you, tens of thousands of Americans have been born and reached their full, God–given potential – because of you.

> As you all know, *Roe vs. Wade* has resulted in some of the most permissive abortion laws anywhere in the world ... The United States is one of only seven countries to allow elective late–term abortions, along with China, North Korea, and others. Right now, in a number of states, the laws allow a baby to be torn from his or her

mother's womb in the ninth month. It is wrong; it has to change ...

He continued:

Americans are more and more pro-life. You see that all the time. In fact, only 12 percent of Americans support abortion on demand at any time. Under my administration, we will always defend the very first right in the Declaration of Independence, and that is the right to life ...

We have just issued a new proposal to protect conscience rights and religious freedoms of doctors, nurses, and other medical professionals. So important ... We are protecting the sanctity of life and the family as the foundation of our society ...

That is why we march. That is why we pray. And that is why we declare that America's future will be filled with goodness, peace, joy, dignity, and life for every child of God.

President Trump began rebuilding the military, allowing them to crush ISIS. He has defended America's allies, such as Israel, from threats by rogue nations. He stated, March 31, 2018:

My fellow Americans, at this holy time of the year, families across our nation gather in homes, churches, and synagogues to light candles and to praise God. During the sacred holiday of Passover, Jewish families around the world give thanks to God for liberating the Jewish people from bondage in Egypt and for delivering them to the Promised Land of Israel.

For Christians, we remember the suffering and death of God's only Son and his glorious resurrection on the third day. On Easter Sunday, we proclaim with joy ...

Christ is Risen!

Both of these sacred celebrations remind us that God's love redeems the world. Almost 3,000 years ago, the prophet Isaiah wrote, "Darkness covers the earth, but the Lord rises upon you and His Glory appears over you. For the Lord will be your everlasting light."

In America, we look to the light of God to guide our steps. We trust in the power of the Almighty for wisdom and strength. And we praise our Heavenly Father for the blessings of freedom and the gift of eternal life ... God bless you and God bless America.

Partnering with prayers of Americans for this miraculous chapter in our history to continue, Trump stated:

• No dream is too big. No challenge is too great. Nothing we want for our future is beyond our reach.

• As President, I will always cherish, honor, and protect the believers who uplift our communities and sustain our nation. To ensure that people of faith can always contribute to our society, my administration has taken historic action to protect religious liberty.

• In America we don't worship government, we worship God.

• When you open your heart to patriotism, there is no room for prejudice. The Bible tells us "How good and pleasant it is for when God's people live together in unity."

℃

CLOSING THOUGHTS

America's history is filled with stories of people who trusted God to use them to improve the world. I pray their lives inspire you at this critical time. America's light still shines despite attacks to turn our republic into a socialist state. We must know the Bible and Constitution and stand for liberty. I challenge you to ask God to lead you to do His will. Let us pray for another true revival in our country – the greatest revival yet! May He lead, guide and protect all Americans, including our President, Congress, judges, and all elected officials, in Jesus Name.

PRAY FOR AMERICA. President Dwight Eisenhower declared:

Our common faith in God is a common bond among us ... As religious faith is the foundation of free government, so is prayer an indispensable part of that faith.

WALK WITH GOD DAILY–BRING OTHERS TO CHRIST. George W. Carver wrote:

Keep your hand in that of the Master, walk daily by His side, so that you may lead others into the realms of true happiness ... which is the "Jesus Way" of life.

CONTRIBUTE YOUR BEST TO YOUR COUNTRY. Eddie Rickenbacker stated:

Thank God I have contributed my best to the land that contributed so much to me.

In closing, may we all still strive for what Lincoln declared in the Gettysburg Address:

That this nation, under God, shall have a new birth of freedom — and that government of the people, by the people, for the people, shall not perish from the earth.

ৎ